WORLD FAMOUS
BATTLES

WORLD FAMOUS
BATTLES

Ian Schott

Constable & Robinson Ltd
3 The Lanchesters
162 Fulham Palace Road
London W6 9ER

This edition published by Magpie Books,
an imprint of Constable & Robinson Ltd 2004

A copy of the British Library Cataloguing in Publication Data
is available from the British Library.

ISBN 1-84529-031-3

Printed and bound in the EU

Contents

Gallipoli

The expedition to the Dardanelles, which led to the disasters and heroism of Gallipoli, was a response to the deadlock on the Western Front. Had the expedition succeeded, it might have changed the course of the whole war; indeed, it might even have forestalled the Bolshevik revolution that was to sweep Russia. But the management of the campaign was unworthy of the courage of the troops who fought and died in vain upon the shores of the Dardanelles.

The background of the conflict lay in the confused sphere of Balkan politics. By 1914, Turkey and its crumbling Ottoman Empire had become the "sick man of Europe". Long ruled by the tyrannical Sultan Abdul Hamid II, its nominal potentate was now Mohammed V. The real power lay in the hands of the legendary "Young Turks", a group of youthful revolutionaries, politicians and outright opportunists. Notable among these was Enver Pasha, a half-Albanian who held the position of War Minister; he had assumed the office by shooting his predecessor.

Drained by its wars in the Balkans, Turkey sought foreign aid. Enver urged an alliance with Germany, and in 1914 a German military mission arrived in Turkey to reorganise the Turkish army. The Germans saw that in the advent of a European war, Turkey occupied a crucial strategic position: her territory straddled the Dardanelles, through which half Russia's grain exports passed, and the route was also Russia's main contact with Britain and France.

Battles

Two days before the outbreak of the Great War, Germany and Turkey signed an alliance against Russia, though Turkey was not as yet committed to military action. But when the British requisitioned two battleships that Turkey had ordered, the Germans seized the opportunity to compensate them with two battle cruisers, thus cementing their military alliance in the eyes of the world. The British withdrew their naval mission and the Germans assumed de facto control of the Turkish Navy. Without reference to the Turkish Government, they closed the Dardanelles to international traffic. Hostilities between the Allies and Turkey officially began on 31 October 1914.

By 1915, the Western Front was deadlocked; lines of opposing trenches ran from the North Sea to Switzerland. In addition, the Allies feared that Russia, reeling from recent reversals and troubled by internal unrest, might collapse unless the pressure on her was relieved.

Winston Churchill (then at the Admiralty) and Lord Kitchener had discussed the possibility of an attack in the Dardanelles; it was to have been launched by Greece but she had since become pro-German. The plan now settled on involved a landing on the Gallipoli peninsula, on the Mediterranean side of the Dardanelles, accompanied by another landing on the Asiatic side of the channel, while the Dardanelles themselves would be "forced" by a fleet of battleships old enough to be spared from service in the west. This fleet would bombard the shore batteries into submission, remove the minefields and secure the straits for the passage of grain and munitions to and from Russia. It was also hoped that this show of force would haul the wavering nations of Greece, Bulgaria and Rumania back into the Allied fold and create a coalition strong enough to crush Turkey.

As Greek assistance was not forthcoming, Kitchener released the 29th Division of the British Army, a regular division of professionals. But four of the divisions to serve at Gallipoli would be Territorials (the 25th and 52nd–54th). Three – the 10th, 11th and 13th – would be units of Kitchener's "New Army" of volunteers. A division consisted of some 18,000 men of all ranks, complemented by around 76 artillery pieces, 48 Vickers machine-guns, 5,000 horses, 834 vehicles and 54 motor vehicles.

Also at Gallipoli were units from the 2nd Mounted Division of Yeomanry, the Royal Naval Division, the Royal Marines, the Indian Brigade, the Gurkha Rifles and the 14th Prince of Wales Own Sikhs. Above all, Gallipoli is synonymous with the Australian and New Zealand Army Corps – the Anzacs – who wore the famous felt slouch hat, the crowns pushed into the "lemon-squeezer" style. Although newly formed and inexperienced (their stiff British officers found them rough and short on discipline), their fighting qualities, physical strength, endurance and sheer courage were awesome; they were perhaps the best troops to fight in the Great War. The substantial French units at Gallipoli were a mixture of native French and French Colonial units.

The Allies faced a Turkish army which, despite the efforts of the Germans, was a haphazard, imperfectly trained conscript army. Men were conscripted for periods of 25 years downwards, of which they could expect to spend two to five in active service; the rest of the time they were theoretically kept in some state of readiness in the reserve. At the outset of the campaign they were ill-equipped, their uniforms and weapons (where available) were poor imitations of old German design, and their divisions were seriously under-strength. Despite these shortcomings, the bulk of the army, drawn from the peasantry of Anatolia, was inured to a life of hardship and possessed an abundance of courage which made them a formidable enemy. The Allies were rashly dismissive about their opponents; by the end of the campaign they had ceased to underrate "Johnny Turk".

The Allies were under the command of Sir Ian Standish Monteith Hamilton, a 62-year-old Scot, appointed by Lord Kitchener, whose deputy he had been in the Boer war. An intelligent, sensitive man with a talent for poetry, Hamilton was renowned for his personal courage, but was generally considered to be too good-natured and considerate for the difficult task he had been handed. Time and again he should have dismissed his inept colleagues, but he lacked the necessary ruthlessness; he chose to advise rather than command, and credited his subordinate generals with too much intelligence.

The Anzacs were under the overall command of 50-year-old Lieutenant-General Sir William Birdwood, undoubtedly one of the best Allied commanders. "Birdie" won the lasting affection of the tough Anzacs. He admired them, and when raised to the peerage insisted on the title "Of Anzacs and Totnes".

The other commanders were a mixed and ill-starred bunch. Lieutenant-General Sir Aylmer Hunter-Western was devoid of imagination, and at times appeared unable to countenance any strategy that did not involve the needless slaughter of his command. Lieutenant-General The Hon. Sir Frederick Stopford, aged 61, had never commanded in battle; a time-server, he was patently inept. Stopford's chief of staff was Brigadier-General Hamilton Reed, the holder of a VC, whose tactical thinking was limited to an insistence on heavy bombardments, which meant that the Allies failed on many occasions to move with necessary speed to consolidate gains.

Whereas ignorance, social niceties, and arrogance beset the English command, the French were afflicted with a corrosive pessimism about the operation. The original French Commander, General Albert d'Amade, had previously been dismissed from his post on the Western Front. He was to crack under the strain of Gallipoli and be replaced by the young, fearless and intelligent Henri Gouraud, one of the best officers in the war, the loss of whom – early in the campaign – proved a dreadful blow. His replacement, the doddering Maurise Bailloud, was hauled out of retirement and impressed on all he met a churlish defeatism.

The Turks were commanded, in effect, by Liman von Sanders, the head of Germany's military mission – a well-organised officer – and the mercurial and inspirational Mustapha Kemal. Though nominally only a divisional commander, Kemal achieved control of the Turkish forces in the peninsula. It was his grasp of strategy – and personal courage – that rallied the Turkish troops.

On 19 February, Vice-Admiral Sackville Carden commenced the naval attack on the Dardanelles, which all hoped would be sufficient to quell the Turks without recourse to an extensive landing by the army. Twelve capital ships in three divisions shelled the forts at the mouth of the channel, Sedd-el-Bahr on the European side and Kum Kale on the Asiatic side. Bad weather rendered the attack ineffective, and it was resumed on 25 February, when the fortifications were battered into submission and occupied. Carden turned his attention to the fortifications 14 miles further up the channel, at "The Narrows" where the strait is less than a mile across. He announced that the navy would be off Constantinople within a fortnight.

This was over-optimistic. The Turks returned to occupy the two forts they had lost. The advance up the channel was halted by extensive minefields, and the shore-batteries began to sink the minesweepers. Under constant pressure from Churchill, Carden had a nervous breakdown and retired from the action. His replacement, Sir John de Roebuck, pressed home the attack in antique fashion on 18

Battles

March, shelling the channel fortifications in broad daylight; his ships made splendid targets for the Turkish gunners, who damaged the superstructure on some of them. Worse was to come, however. A Turkish mine expert had laid a discreet chain of 20 mines parallel to the Asiatic shore – not across the Channel as the attacking navy expected. By 4 p.m., as the incessant pounding from the great, creaking cruisers had all but silenced the guns of Chanak and Kilid Bahr, the French cruiser *Bouvet* hit a mine and immediately sank. Then HMS *Inflexible* hit a mine and began to take on water; within minutes HMS *Irresistible* hit another and was devoured by the coastal waters. The catastrophe was completed when HMS *Ocean* hit a mine, lost her steering gear and sank.

The losses were sufficient to persuade Hamilton – perhaps incorrectly – that victory by a naval assault was impossible. Despite the sunken and damaged ships, the shore defences had been subdued, the Turks were low on ammunition, the principal minefields could now be cleared and more ships were on the way; had they pressed home the naval assault they might very well have run through to Constantinople. But the massive landings were now scheduled to proceed.

Confusion reigned from the start. There was no supreme commander, army and naval forces remaining instead under independent leadership; forces were scattered and ill-equipped, and intelligence was poor. Hamilton said he could not mount an attack before mid-April. Surprise was therefore lost and Liman von Sanders had every opportunity to reorganise the Turkish defences.

He deployed some 80,000 men in six divisions. Two of these were stationed on the Asiatic coast near Kum Kale. He identified four possible landing sites on the Gallipoli peninsula itself and distributed the remainder of his forces to cover these: Bulair at the north; Suvla, midway on the western shore of the peninsula; Ari Burnu in the south; and Cape Helles at the tip of the peninsula. Each of these possible landings was overlooked by high ground: Helles lay in the shadow of Achi Baba hill, Ari Burnu was overlooked by the Sari Bair ridge, and Suvla by the Tekke Tepe ridge. Mustapha Kemal waited in reserve with a division. Von Sanders also had time to deploy his limited supplies of land-mines and barbed wire.

Including the French divisions, Hamilton had at his disposal nearly 75,000 men, of whom 30,500 were Anzacs. It was to be the greatest amphibious landing ever attempted, on six beaches: Ari Burnu, where the Anzacs were to land (forever known simply as Anzac or Anzac Cove), and beaches designated S, V, W, X and Y.

Little was known about the Ari Burnu area other than that it was a small beach, hemmed in by precipitous cliffs; a bleak, threatening landscape. In the early dawn of 25 April, the first Anzacs went ashore from their small boats. They found themselves almost completely unopposed, and bayoneted the few defenders. The terrain was more inhospitable than expected. The beach was only yards wide and the cliffs and gullies offered no cover. When day broke, they saw they had landed at the wrong beach. Strong currents had swept them nearly a mile north of their designated landing spot. They continued to come ashore, and tried to establish a bridge-head on the minute beach. The terrain inland was too steep to allow any co-ordinated advance, and innumerable skirmishes with the straggling Turks further hindered their confused progress. In the meantime – in a move which may well have decided the course of the campaign – Kemal force-marched his reserve division towards Anzac Cove. He did not attack the beach-head, but wisely saw that in this terrain the side that held the high ground – and thus commanded the Narrows – would win the conflict. He established himself on the heights of Sari Bair and Chunuk Bair, above Anzac Cove. The Anzacs, whose unexpected landing had threatened the whole central portion of the peninsula, now faced fortified high ground. A resolute counter-attack by Kemal's force prevented the Anzacs from rushing the ridge until the defences had been established. Amid bitter hand-to-hand fighting, the Turks won a crucial moment in the campaign.

Meanwhile, four miles up the coast from the tip of Cape Helles at Y beach, Hamilton landed 2,000 Scottish Borderers and Marines in an attempt to take the defenders in the rear and then link up with the main assault force around Cape Helles. The attackers found themselves dumped, not on a beach, but on a 200-foot cliff with a few awful eyries to cling to. They clawed up the cliff, but having reached the top received no further orders. The chain of command began to unravel. Hamilton started the day as he was to spend the campaign – sitting offshore in the *Queen Elizabeth*. He sailed past Y beach, but apologetically said that he could not put more men ashore to capitalise on the advantage, as he would be interfering with Hunter-Western's command. A few of the Marines became bored and went for a stroll. They reached the heights of Krithia, which they found deserted. Hunter-Western was entirely engrossed in his pre-planned landings further south, and would not authorise the occupation of these vital strategic positions – the attempted capture of which would later cost thousands of lives. The Marines went back to the cliff-top.

At X, W, and V beaches, which ran anti-clockwise around the tip of Cape Helles, the initial landings were entrusted to Fusiliers of the 29th Division. At X beach, a strip of sand 200 yards long and backed with a 40-foot escarpment, the Fusiliers found only 12 defenders; after overcoming some stiffer resistance inland, they were able to link up with forces on the adjoining W beach.

On W beach the Turks were well dug in with machine-guns and barbed wire. The heroic British assault by the 1st Lancashire Fusiliers has become part of regimental history. Waves of men poured ashore in the face of withering fire; hundreds were mown down, but their gallantry won them six VCs before breakfast. They stormed the gun emplacements in an operation which Hamilton believed was unsurpassed in the annals of military history. But, like so much of the Gallipoli operation, such casualties need not have occurred had Hamilton and others been alert to the opportunities elsewhere.

At V beach, ships bombarded the Turkish positions at daybreak. Then the collier, *River Clyde*, packed to the gunwales with troops, and with special landing apertures cut in her sides, was deliberately run aground. In theory a series of lighters were to be moored to provide a bridge to the shore for the soldiers. But the Turks had survived the initial bombardment, and now returned fire. The men who had landed in advance of the main party were compelled to take shelter or were mown down; the sea turned red with blood fifty yards from the shore. It was impossible to get the lighters in position and the troops remained trapped inside the *River Clyde*. Not until nightfall was the main bulk of the force able to land. The débâcle was another ill-conceived plan by the upper echelons of the army; once again, it was only through the courage and discipline of the soldiers that it was prevented from becoming a wholesale massacre.

At S Beach, where the naval bombardment had a much greater effect, the landing was accomplished with speed and an imagination lacking elsewhere. The troops were dug in by nightfall. The French landed, with some initial uncertainty, across the straits at Kum Kale, to prevent the British landings coming under artillery fire from the fortifications.

By the end of the day, despite a shortage of landing craft and horrendous casualties, the Allies had 30,000 troops ashore. At Cape Helles, the Turkish defences had been largely shattered, suffering 1,000 casualties, half their forces. It was a time to push forward, before Kemal could reinforce the high points in the pensula; a night-strike inland from Cape Helles would unite the British with the hard-pressed Anzacs by dawn, encircling and destroying the Turkish defence within days. But, anchored offshore, the officers failed to appreciate the situation, and chose to dig in rather than capitalise on their significant gains. By the morning of 26 April, the confused landing at Y beach was over. The lack of clear instructions, combined with a reluctance to delegate responsibility to the forces there, created a situation in which the Borderers, whose Colonel had been killed, were evacuated and the Marines were not informed. The Marines fought off the Turks and, having gained this advantage, discovered that since the Borderers had left they had no option but to evacuate.

At Anzac, matters were worse. Crammed onto a beach a half-mile long and only 30 yards wide, the Anzacs who had established a bridge-head only 1,200 yards deep, were now subject to repeated, violent counter-attacks by Kemal's Turks, sweeping down from the heights above the beach. The Turks suffered 2,000 casualties and were weakening when Birdwood, at the instigation of his divisional commanders, asked Hamilton for permission to evacuate. After deliberation, he told the Anzacs to dig in and "stick it out". All surprise and impetus had now been lost and the invasion turned into a war of attrition, in which troops at beach-heads would survive in shallow holes scraped in the barren earth. Over the following days, the Anzacs fought with the bayonet to keep their precarious grip on the peninsula, and within 24 hours the 1st Australian Division sustained some 4,500 casualties.

As the Anzacs dug in, their trenches and bolt-holes were often only five yards from the Turkish line. Each bush, crag,

THE BATTLE OF THE MARNE 1914. Five German Armies surged forward into France from Amiens to Verdun in late August 1914. They were confronted by French forces and the British Expeditionary Force (BEF). After the French withdrew to defend Paris, the Allies retreated to a line south of the Seine. A change in the German attack exposed their plan and the French 6th Army, under Maunoury, commandeered 600 Paris taxis to make an opportunist attack. The other Allied forces did not hear of the tactical switch and continued to fall back; the British reversed back into the action the following day. The Germans withdrew. On 8 September they launched a counter-attack at the centre of the line which threw back the French under Marshal Foch. The battle swung one way and another until the German command ordered a generel retreat. It was the last chance – for both sides – to bring a quick end to the Great War on the Western Front. Casualties were dreadful: 800,000 Germans and and over a million French and British.

gully and rock concealed huge numbers of men and took on enormous strategic significance; quantities of blood were shed over a few inches of dust. Plagues of bloated flies thrived on the thousands of decomposing corpses. The Anzacs were assailed by dysentery. Moreover, their equipment was unsuited to the terrain. They had few trench mortars, and hand grenades had not been thought necessary; the Anzacs and British began manufacturing grenades from empty jam-tins.

Battles

Short of water, and under constant attack from snipers, the Anzacs still played cricket on the beach. Despite the bitter fighting, the Anzacs and Turks generally treated each other's prisoners and wounded well, and would arrange truces to allow the necessary collection and burial of the dead. The Anzacs quickly concluded that "Johnny Turk" was no unprincipled heathen, but a "good, clean fighter".

On 26 April, the fortfications at Sedd-el-Bahr on Cape Helles were captured and X, W, V and S beaches were linked up, to leave the tip of the peninsula in Allied hands. The French had been driven off Kum Kale (now no great strategic loss) and their forces joined up with Hamilton's army. Hamilton now ordered that the heights of Achi Baba should be taken, and on 28 April, under the command of Hunter-Western, the first battle of Krithia was joined. By mid-morning, hampered by the difficult terrain and Hunter-Western's lack of co-ordination, the attacking force of 14,000 had suffered 3,000 casualties.

Hamilton needed ammunition and reinforcements to continue such attacks. He believed that Kitchener had told him that there would be no further troops. In a fearful cock-up wholly in keeping with the conduct of the Great War, Kitchener had mentioned to the British commander in Egypt, Sir John Maxwell, that he was to let Hamilton have what troops could be spared from the garrison there. Since Hamilton had not been told about this arrangement, he did not request the troops; since Maxwell did not hear from him, he believed that the troops were not required. It was only when the Admiralty heard news of the campaign's lack of progress that Kitchener appreciated that the reinforcements were needed.

When Hamilton heard they were coming, he dug in and waited, which once again gave von Sanders the opportunity to reorganise. On 1 May, the Turks launched an assault on the Allied line right across the peninsula. They

12

gave up after terrible losses, but the Allied forces also suffered heavy casualties.

When the reinforcements arrived, Hamilton switched around and reconstituted some of his shattered brigades, and made another assault on Achi Baba – the second battle of Krithia, which was fought between 6 and 8 May. On the heights, the troops faced barbed wire and Turkish machine-gunners. Hamilton suggested to Hunter-Western that he might make resistance more difficult by attacking at night. Hunter-Western differed; the attacks continued in daylight, with predictable slaughter. By the time the assault was called off, 600 yards had been gained at a cost of 6,500 casualties. Australians, borrowed from Anzac Cove, fought with peerless courage, suffering up to 40% casualties; when their officers fell, they did not cease to fight, but NCOs or even enlisted men would take over command and continue the battle.

Hamilton faced a stalemate. He pleaded for more divisions. Instead, a resumption of the naval attack was discussed in London, but a political crisis, which resulted in the removal of Churchill from the Admiralty, ensured that Hamilton was left to fend for himself. He switched the emphasis from a drive up the peninsula to a major offensive at Anzac Cove. First, however, he had to capture Achi Baba.

The Turks threw their troops at Anzac Cove, where the Australians and New Zealanders held out against massed attacks by up to 30,000 men. On one such assault, on 19 May, the Turks suffered nearly 10,000 casualties to the Anzacs' 100 dead and 500 wounded.

On 24 May, Hamilton promoted Hunter-Western to Lieutenant-General and gave him control of all the British forces at Helles. Along with the French General Gouraud, Hunter-Western planned another assault on Achi Baba, the third battle of Krithia, which began on 4 June. Some 30,000 British and French troops, supported by artillery, attacked

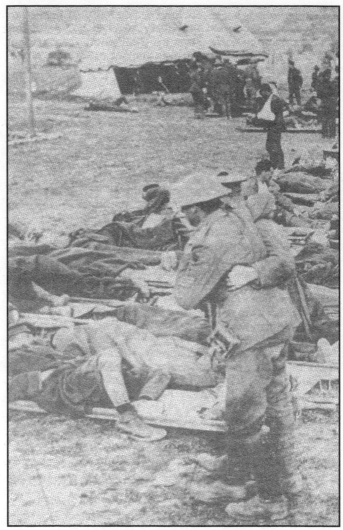

A field dressing team, 1916

25,000 well dug-in Turks. Despite early gains by the French, the operation, conducted in broad daylight, was another costly failure. Murderous crossfire from Turkish machine-gunners cost the British 4,000 casualties. In the aftermath, while Hamilton contemplated his ravaged forces, the Turks strengthened their fortifications.

It was trench warfare no different from the Western Front. In London, the Dardanelles Committee, set up to run the campaign, quarrelled over tactics. Within Turkish waters, a notably successful war was fought by British submarines, which caused much consternation to the Turkish and German authorities, sinking ships and landing saboteurs. It demonstrated the considerable advantages of a swifter, more mobile campaign, with better strategic preparations.

Kitchener finally agreed to dispatch three of his "New Army" divisions to Gallipoli. While awaiting their arrival, the Allies passed June in a state of fractious torpor, with constant fire-fights and probing attacks between the two sides. Water was now in desperately short supply; most of it had to come from Egypt. In heat which melted all their tinned supplies, men were rationed to a dangerous three pints of water per day. While short of food and munitions, the Turks had a plentiful supply of spring water.

Hamilton stayed offshore, and then moved to the Greek Island of Imbros, where he saw none of the horrors of the peninsula. In late June and early July, Hunter-Western pushed the depleted and exhausted British and French once more towards Achi Baba. A few yards of blood-soaked trenches were gained at a cost of nearly 8,000 casualties (the Turks lost twice that number). It was a futile exercise, lacking in compassion. In the case of the Royal Naval Division, the commanding officer described the action as "a wicked and useless slaughter of men". On 20 July, Hunter-Western fell ill and returned, unlamented, to Britain.

Battles

Hamilton's reinforcements arrived under the control of the elderly and infirm Lieutenant-General Stopford – a lethal choice considering the inexperienced nature of his troops, a mixture of volunteers and Territorials. It was decided to land these at Suvla Bay, five miles north of Anzac Cove. The attack would turn the Turkish flank and allow the Anzacs to break out and take the vital Sari Bair ridge.

The landings were planned for 6 August, when the Turks were to be diverted by attacks at Anzac and Helles. The diversion at Helles was fruitless and wasteful. At Anzac, the forces were secretly reinforced with 13,000 men slipped ashore in the dead of night. With part of his 40,000 men, Birdwood launched an attack on the Turkish positions via a secret tunnel; the main body was to quietly move northwards against Sari Bair. The diversionary attack was led by 1 Australian Brigade, whose force of 2,900 suffered 1,700 casualties in desperate hand-to-hand fighting against greater Turkish forces; they nevertheless took the area known as "Lone Pine", winning seven VCs. No less heroic was the Australian Light Horse, who responded to orders which condemned them to futile and suicidal attacks with immeasurable gallantry; wave after wave of the horsemen attacked uphill against Turkish defences north of Lone Pine. Nearly three-quarters of the 60-strong cavalry was destroyed within fifteen minutes.

The intended break-out to Sari Bair also ended in failure. Once more, the sheer courage of the troops took them to within yards of their objectives. But the incompetence of their English leaders and a critical lack of communication resulted in almost complete annihilation of some companies of the Anzacs – particularly the New Zealanders, who, stranded on the bleak landscape, fought the Turkish counter-attacks to the last man.

Also involved were elements of the Loyal North

Lancashire and Wiltshire Regiments, who relieved the shattered New Zealanders of the precious high ground they had taken and, as Hamilton wrote, "died where they stood". The 1/6th Gurkhas, who had distinguished themselves in the hand-to-hand fighting, were the last to retreat. The action cost 12,000 casualties.

At Suvla, the troops began landing during the late evening of 6 August. Hamilton was at Imbros, and Stopford anchored offshore, so neither had a first-hand view of the débâcle they had precipitated. The landing was to take place on three beaches: A, B and C. As at Anzac, many were landed on the wrong beaches, and those who were deposited correctly were uncertain as to their objectives. They had, at this point, a considerable advantage over the small force of Turkish defenders; despite the deplorable execution of the operation, the design was sound, and the door was wide open for Stopford to sweep inland and turn the course of the wretched Gallipoli campaign.

But a rapid advance to secure important objectives on the high ground was impossible, because no one had a clear idea of the geography of the region. Stopford was content to signal to Hamilton that he had got most of his troops ashore; Hamilton had given him few orders beyond this, and duly signalled back that the old buffer had done "splendidly". By 7 August, only one of the hills overlooking the landing area had been assailed and taken, and Stopford, resting a sprained leg, had still not gone ashore. Somewhat perplexed, Hamilton visited Suvla; Stopford genteelly declined to accompany him onto the beach.

Ashore, Hamilton realised the dreadful situation; a position of potential victory was now becoming another killing ground. Liman von Sanders had marshalled his defences, and appointed Mustapha Kemal to overall command. By the time the British organised a general attack on 9 August, the Turks were reinforced and waiting.

Battles

As the British scaled the heights, they found the Turks digging in on the previously unoccupied ground; the two days of delay had cost them the war. In the midst of the battle, Hamilton, looking for Stopford, encountered him supervising the construction of a personal dug-out, seemingly oblivious to his responsibilities.

The Suvla landing was another dead end. Within days, 18,000 casualties had been sustained for no advantage. Yet a wave of further, vain assaults were launched at Suvla. In one of these the entire 1/5th Norfolk Regiment vanished, never to be seen again.

Hamilton's command structure began to collapse as his generals fell to quarrelling. He asked Kitchener to replace Stopford; Kitchener said that he was dispatching three generals – Byng, Maude and Fanshawe – from the Western Front. Hamilton sacked Stopford and replaced him with Major-General de Lisle, under whom Lieutenant-General Sir Brian Mahon refused to serve on the grounds that de Lisle was his inferior in rank. Mahon duly abandoned his division in the midst of battle, and his parting was accompanied by that of the broken Major-General Hammersley, for whom it had all proved too much.

Hamilton transferred elements of the illustrious 29th Division from Helles to Suvla, to spearhead one last punch. The attack was largely unsuccessful, and over a third of the 14,300 men participating became casualties, principally from Turkish shelling. By the end of August, Anzac and Suvla had been linked through the efforts of the Anzacs, but thereafter, with both sides exhausted, the Dardanelles campaign lapsed into sporadic forays and sniping.

In London and Australia, public opinion was swelling against the continuation of the fruitless battle for the peninsula. The Austrian Prime Minister complained to the British Government about the handling of the campaign. The Turks had also suffered. Half their entire army was on

THE BATTLES OF AISNE: 1914, 1917 AND 1918.
In September 1914, the Germans, having lost the
first battle of the Marne, retreated to a strong high
position on the plateau north of the Aisne river,
and dug in for trench warfare. Unaware of this
change of tactics, the Allied Armies, under Generel
Joffre, conducted a frontal assault. Having crossed
the Aisne by pontoon bridges, they assaulted
strong German positions, but were then flung back
to their starting point. After another failed assault,
the battle dwindled out into the trench warfare
that would charecterise the war. In April 1917,
General Nivelle ordered an attack by two French
Armies along a 50-mile stretch of the Aisne in
Champagne. Entrenched on the northern slopes of
the river, the Germans knocked out 150 French
tanks and then counter-attacked. After a month of
fighting, the French were exhausted, and had
suffered 100,000 casualties. Defeatism and mutiny
erupted; 28,385 were found guilty and 55 were
shot. Had not the Americans intervened, the
French might well have sought peace with
Germany. The third battle of the Marne came a
year later, in May 1918. Against a now thinly held
Allied front, the Germans launched a ferocious
bombardment and then sent in 41 divisions. The
British clung on to their sector, but the French
were forced back 35 miles. The Germans took
55,000 prisoners and 450 guns before American
troops marched in to staunch the flow, capturing
Cantigny and Bellau Wood. The British were then
able to counter-attack.

the tiny peninsula, and they were trying to solicit America's help in bringing the war to an end.

The Dardanelles Committee conferred; ravaged by battle and disease, the Allied forces awaited the judgement. Hamilton, reluctant to give up, said that an evacuation would cost the lives of half his troops; instead, he asked for more men. But he lost two divisions who were called away to face Bulgaria, and was then sacked and replaced by General Sir Charles Munro (Kitchener opposed this – he had at last seen the light and wanted Birdwood appointed Supreme Commander). On arrival, Munro, fresh from the Western Front, visited Suvla, Anzac and Helles in a single day, giving the situation little more than cursory consideration before recommending a withdrawal. Birdwood believed success was still possible. Kitchener was dispatched to have a look. It was the first visit he had paid. He found the peninsula "an awful place". He ordered a withdrawal, initially from Anzac and Suvla. Helles should be maintained for a time. Birdwood supervised the evacuation and it was unquestionably the best managed operation of the whole campaign.

As winter arrived, both armies were afflicted by blizzards, frostbite and floods. They dug in deeper, neither side imagining that the campaign was over. Then on 12 December, the troops of Anzac and Suvla were informed that they were to be taken off. To conceal this from the Turks, empty supply boxes continued to be ferried ashore, and as the troops were silently evacuated under cover of darkness the usual number of camp-fires were lit. The artillery continued to shell the Turkish lines. By 18 December, 40,000 men had been removed, half of the total forces at Anzac and Suvla. By 19 December, another 20,000 had slipped away, leaving only 20,000 facing the Turks, who, had they discovered the weakness of the force now facing them, could have massacred at will. But forethought and discipline ensured success. On the night of 19 December, the remaining troops fell back to the beaches along pre-arranged routes. They left in their wake a series of mines, booby traps and guns which, along with weapons which had been rigged with weights and water to fire automatically, were intended to convince the Turks that the front trenches were still occupied. By dawn, the Turks, finding the front line strangely quiet, began to wade over the barbed wire and clamber into the enemy trenches. They found the beaches utterly deserted; an army of 80,000 had vanshed. The evacuation was accomplished without fatalities; only two men were slightly wounded.

When Liman von Sanders realised what had happened, he mustered the 21 divisions at his disposal for a crushing assault on Helles. The Allies had hoped to maintain the position there pending further deliberations; fearing a massacre, they now decided to evacuate the four divisions immediately. Munro returned to the Western Front, and it was left to Birdwood, again, to ensure a phased withdrawal.

There were 40,000 men at Helles. By 7 January, only 19,000 were still ashore. It was now that von Sanders threw his overwhelmingly superior forces into the attack. But the assault, which should have annihilated the Allied forces, failed almost immediately in the face of resolute British fire. Mustapha Kemal had long since retired from the campaign, mentally exhausted, and, after months of heroic defence, his Turkish soldiers had nothing further to offer. They fell back, and refused to advance. This last engagement cost the Allies only 164 casualties, principally from heavy shelling. The evacuation continued, using the same deceptions as at Anzac and Suvla. Not a further man was lost.

At 4 a.m. on 9 January 1916, the British ammunition dumps along the Helles shoreline exploded spectacularly, lighting up the black winter sky. The Turks roused themselves from the dug-outs and, mistaking the sound for incoming fire, dutifully launched a counter-bombardment. The shells landed on empty beaches. The troops of the doomed Dardanelles Expedition – the Gallipoli Campaign – were all offshore, rocking on the cold sea, which would take them off to face the horror of the Somme. The battle cost the lives of at least 87,000 Turks, who were mostly shovelled by their fellows into pits and ravines, and whose individual acts of courage were little recorded (there is only one Turkish war grave on the peninsula). About 47,000 British, French, Australians, New Zealanders and Indians died; their graveyards are dotted all over the peninsula, for conditions tended to result in the dead being buried where they fell. Hamilton never again commanded in the field. Mustapha Kemal became, in time, Kemal Ataturk, the founding father of modern Turkey.

Chapter Two

The Somme

When the First World War broke out, the British Army was a small, professional force. By the end of 1914, Lord Kitchener's appeal for volunteers had swelled the ranks to near unmanageable proportions. Each town and borough throughout the nation, swept by patriotic fervour, raised its own brigade of volunteers. Few of them had military experience. Though attached to regular army divisions, they remained "Kitchener's Army", and in many cases, young men from specific localities remained together as "Pals" brigades.

They were fiercely patriotic, enthusiastic and convinced that they were involved in a just fight in which victory would be swift. Without weapons or experienced officers, they drilled on village greens with broom handles under the nervous eye of men given rank because their experience in the cadets – or even the Boy Scouts – gave them some knowledge of organisation. The British Army was wholly oriented around the principle of unquestioning discipline, and the volunteers were ceaselessly drilled until they acquired the standards of polish and instinctive obedience demanded; they were trained to be dependent on the continuous receipt of precise and detailed military instructions.

Although they had no experience of battle, there was no means by which they could be slowly blooded. For thousands, their first and last taste of warfare would be the final seconds between leaving their trenches and the moment that they fell, caught by a bullet or tossed to the winds by shellfire. Half a million of these volunteers came to the gently rolling landscape of Picardy, and took up positions in the woods, fields and farming hamlets inland from the towns of Amiens and Albert.

Sweeping forward over the Belgian frontier, driving the French and British back in a series of great and bloody battles, the Germans first came to the future battlefield of the Somme at the end of September 1914. By the summer of 1916, the Germans had turned the Somme front into an almost impregnable line of fortifications; a double line of trenches protected by a savage steel jungle of barbed wire. To gain the greatest advantage offered by the natural defensive contours of the landscape, their line hugged every slope, depression and ravine. Every wood, hilltop and building had been utilised and fortified for observation, concealment and defence. The trees bristled with machine-guns and artillery; farms were citadels and each village a fortress. They had built massive concrete structures at key points and had tunnelled far beneath their trenches to build a system of galleries and shelters so deep that the most ferocious of bombardments would have little effect. If the Germans could have chosen a place to meet a frontal assault, it would have been the Somme.

The front line between the German and Allied forces stretched from Ypres in the north via Loos, Lens and Arras, to Albert on the River Ancre. The French forces were hopelessly over-extended, along a 400-mile front line, and were suffering catastrophic losses at Verdun. The British took over the French-manned front line along the Somme sector, and faced the Germans in an arc from Heputerne, to the banks of the River Somme.

The French needed the British to launch an assault which would soak up German reserves and relieve the pressure their own forces were under at Verdun, where they were to lose 200,000 men. For political reasons, a joint attack by

French and British forces was planned, at the point where the two armies linked, south of the Somme. But, while the British forces available at the Somme sector continued to swell, the French forces ebbed away at Verdun. The burden of any attack increasingly fell on the British forces; they would be expected to thrust directly across this most heavily fortified sector of the German line.

The co-ordination of the Allied effort was a delicate matter. The confused command structure, politics and personal and national rivalries among the officer corps contributed to the disasters of the First World War; the situation desperately required the firm authority of one individual who possessed the trust of all parties. Sir Douglas Haig, appointed Commander-in-Chief of the British Forces in France, did not relish the choice of battlefield (he wanted a British assault on the north of the front line). There was little he could do; the political forces at work possessed too great a momentum. A big push was expected at the Somme, and it would therefore take place.

After months of planning, decoy activity, entrenchment and the secret mining of German fortifications, the objectives were fixed; the British would attack at the end of June over a 15-mile front, using 18 divisions, and head for the town of Bapaume in the Germans' rear. To the south, the French would attack with 16 divisions; their objective was Peronne.

Haig had 150,000 men ready to go over the top. The army overcame phenomenal logistical problems to assemble, encamp and equip the flood of troops into the area. The narrow country roads made troop movements a slow business requiring detailed timetables to avoid collisions; a single brigade and its support staff on the move could occupy three miles of road, and take two and a half hours to pass that distance.

In addition to the natural defensive positions the

Germans occupied, the British infantry faced a triple line of defences which extended up to eight kilometres to the rear of the front line. Each line of defences was built around a chain of pillboxes – machine-gun posts surrounded by acres of barbed wire. The destruction of the barbed wire was of the greatest importance. The assault was to be preceded by an intense artillery barrage, which would in theory cut a swathe through the barbed wire and simultaneously obliterate the Germans' forward positions, burying the soldiers in their trenches, destroying emplacements and razing the woodland in which they had concealed themselves.

After an initial heavy barrage, the infantry attack would proceed according to a timetable determined by a series of artillery barrage "lifts". The infantry would be allocated a precise number of minutes to reach the German front line; the artillery barrage would then "lift" from that line to the next line of enemy defences; they would shell for a predetermined period, during which the infantry were expected to reach this objective; the barrage would again be "lifted" further inland. If the artillery prevailed the infantry would stroll in and mop up the few remaining Germans. It was thought that nobody would survive the intended barrage.

The timing of the "lifts" was worked out in exercises to the rear of the British line. The officers timed the simulated attacks with stop-watches and made generous allowances for battlefield conditions. Three things could go wrong. If a friendly troop ran ahead of the timetable, he would be exposed to the shellfire. If the troops did not keep up with the timetable, the advantage won by the barrage would be lost if the Germans regrouped. The barrage could prove ineffective. This last was considered impossible; but all three would happen.

On Saturday, 24 June 1916, the initial bombardment

THE BATTLES OF YPRES: 1914, 1915 AND 1917. In the last major engagement of 1914, the Germans under General von Falkenhayn attacked the British Expeditionary Force (BEF) at Ypres, where the British were linked to the Belgians. They advanced several miles before French reinforcements and the Belgian decision to flood their front line halted them. The British held the ruins of Ypres. Nearly 80% of the original BEF died at Ypres – some 58,000 officers and men. The French lost 50,000, the Germans over 130,000. The next April, the Germans attacked again, this time using chlorine gas; thousands of British died on the four-mile front. Despite further gas attacks, Canadian reserves repulsed the Germans. The British drew back to the ruins of Ypres, which they held at the bitter cost of some 60,000 casualties. The Germans lost 35,000. Two years later, in June 1917, British and New Zealand troops used 19 buried mines to blow a hole in the German defences. After a ten-day bombardment, the British advanced for two days before the attack foundered as torrential rain turned the battlefield into a bloody quagmire. Thereafter, limited advances of a few miles were achieved. Finally, on 20 September, Canadian and Australians took Passchendaele (as the third battle of Ypres is also known). The six months fighting cost the British a staggering 240,000 men, for a gain of five miles.

Battles

began. It could be heard 70 miles away at Montreuil, the Headquarters of the British Army. Unprecedented quantities of high explosive were hurled at the German forces: 150,000 rounds a day. The field guns shot until their recoil buffers gave in, or their breeches were red-hot and had to be struck open with axes. The churches, farms and genteel homes of the countryside were reduced to powder. Woods became barren fields, and green fields turned to cratered and ravined landscapes. The Germans cowered in their deep shelters, driven half-insane and deafened by the hellish noise and vibrations.

The weather, which had been fine at the start of the barrage, enabling observers and spotter aircaft to target the guns and assess damage, began to turn cold and showery. Bad visibility delayed the assault by 48 hours, and the artillery redoubled the onslaught on the German barbed-wire entanglements. Progress was haphazard. Many of the gunners were inexperienced and the munitions were unreliable – the time fuses, which detonated the shrapnel shells above the wire, were either set incorrectly or failed to ignite. Many of the shells simply buried themselves in the mud. It took enormous concentrated firepower to cut a single consistent gap in the wire. Such gaps as were created assisted the Germans. They anticipated that it was into these narrow channels that the British would flood, and positioned their machine-guns accordingly.

The Germans sat out the barrage for five days and nights, without sleep, food and often without water. Their communications were frequently cut and their casualties high. As the British troops gathered in the assembly trenches, they were cheered by the intelligence reports their officers read to them – there was every reason to believe that the enemy was demoralised and all but destroyed. Each man was laden down with 60 pounds of equipment, plus spades, pickaxes and rolls of barbed wire with which to consolidate the positions they would take by nightfall.

On the morning of 1 July a gentle mist spread over the ravaged countryside, presaging a fine, hot day ahead. The British had for several days been carrying out decoy tactics at the northern end of the battlefront, near the village of Gommecourt, in order to convince the Germans that it was here that the main thrust of the attack could be expected. As the British artillery wound up for a final frenzied barrage, the German guns plastered the area north and south of Gommecourt.

The first British move took place at 7.20 a.m. While other units crept forward to the edge of the wire, and raised their scaling ladders to the edge of the dewy parapets, British engineers exploded a vast mine they had tunnelled into position under German fortifications on the "Hawthorn" Redoubt, north of Thiepval. A vast fountain of earth shot 100 feet into the air. As the shock waves ebbed away, machine-gunners rushed forward to secure the gaping crater. In the aftermath of the explosion, a terrible silence fell. It lasted for ten minutes, until the main attack began.

Down the southern end of the line, where the French and British units met, a ferocious mortar assault on the German lines appeared to have utterly depopulated them. The French and British grinned cheerfully at each other, and some even linked arms, preparing to cross No Man's Land.

At 7.30 a.m. the whistles blew. As the mist cleared and the sun burned down, 100,000 men rose and, extended in companies 100 paces apart, began to advance across the churned fields of Picardy towards the distant, silent German lines.

Night fell early on the Somme, the summer evening dimmed by the dust and smoke of battle, while the sunset was shattered by the false dawn of yellow light flashing from the sooty mouths of 3,000 heavy pieces of artillery ranged along the horizon. Long, ragged clouds of evil smoke and gas shrouded the hills. The earth shuddered, groaned and mutated ceaselessly.

At interludes in the shelling, a strange insistent noise, emanating from No Man's Land, raised the hairs of those British still within their trenches. It was the sound of the wounded and dying, lying in the darkness. There were 150,000 men out there.

The first wave of troops had marched, almost unopposed, into the first line of German trenches, and had triumphantly raised their markers to signal their progress. But there they had stayed. For the Germans had risen from the deep shelters of their second line and cut them down.

Along the many decimated divisions, the 31st Division, composed of "Pals" brigades, south of Gommecourt, had lost two out of every three men who had walked out into the maelstrom. The 1st and 4th Tyneside Scottish had been annihilated, and every single colonel had perished at the head of his battalion.

Tommies who had managed to survive found themselves cut off, without ammunition, bombs or any prospect of relief. They fought fiercely with the bayonet – when they had the opportunity to engage the Germans at close quarters. But for the most part they lost the little ground they took. The few significant gains were to the south. Elsewhere the attack had completely failed.

The troops had also found that even their weapons were ineffectual. Those in the second wave, told they were going into the German trenches to "mop up", dutifully hurled their Mills bombs into the dug-outs and trenches, only to find that the bombs would explode before reaching the ground. They swept on regardless and were then cut to pieces from the rear by Germans who had emerged unscathed from their deep warrens.

The troops had been trained for a successful assault, and

Gunners at Fricourt, Mametz Valley

had no idea what to do when things went wrong. They had been trained to obey orders, and now all their officers were dead. They had been trained to move as an army, and scattered individuals were all that was left.

The silence that had fallen after the mine had been detonated at "Hawthorn" Redoubt was a monstrous error. The bombardment should have continued; the sudden silence gave the Germans warning of the intended attack. They had a vital ten minutes to crawl out of their dug-outs, man the machine-guns, train them on the channels in the barbed wire and bring their artillery to bear.

At British Headquarters, conflicting reports poured in. The attendant press, expecting a triumphant day, awaited official news of the battle. Matters were alternately described as "generally favourable . . . our losses slight . . . a methodical and well-disciplined advance . . . effective progress . . .". In reality, though one or two copses and hamlets had changed hands, the battlefield was static. If nothing had been taken, where then, the staff officers asked, were all the soldiers? There were mutterings that some divisions – including the 8th up at Gommecourt – must have failed to attack. But the evidence of a massacre was soon piling up at the field hospitals.

By the morning, the extent of the losses began to become clear: there were 57,000 officers and men dead and wounded – all these for barely 1,000 yards of mud.

Sombre and tentative, Haig and his generals assessed the possibilities for the following day. They must persist; they must hold the line at its northern extent, take Thiepval and capitalise on their modest gains in the south.

The reserve divisions went over the top. Among those who advanced towards la Boiselle – where the previous day the front line German trenches had been taken – were battalions of the Wiltshire Regiment, part of the 19th Division. Their objective was still the second line of German trenches. But the third line of Germans, dug in on higher ground, had a comprehensive view of the action. Not only were they able to call down artillery fire with great precision; they had taken the opportunity to fix the traverse angles on their heavy machine-guns to create a withering crossfire which cut down men as they rose above the parapets.

The 10th Worcesters were also massacred: 810 men walked across the mud and barbed wire; 428 came out. But they took the third line of trenches in bitter hand-to-hand fighting with bayonet and gun-butt, though they lost their commanding officer.

Over the next few days, the assaults and counter-assaults continued, each one gaining a few yards and bleeding the British forces further. In No Man's Land the thousands of dead lay unburied, their corpses decomposing, blackening in the rain and sun.

Haig accepted that the attack had failed, and settled for a war of attrition; for ten weeks the Allies hammered the German lines. But even the first tank attack of the war, on 15 September, failed to dislodge the Germans. On 18 November, the battle spluttered out. The British Government could not countenance the loss of any more lives in such a vain effort (Lord Lansdowne, after visiting the battlefield, had cabled the Cabinet: "Are we going to continue until we have killed ALL our young men?").

On 27 September, two years after the Germans had moved in, Thiepval fell to the British. When the Germans had come, it was a rural idyll. Now, a few scattered chips of brick marked the church and the chateau had vanished but for a small pile of grey stones. There was not a tree, not a blade of grass. Through the mist, the barren, poisoned land was covered with bodies. The latter had fought to the death to hold a village that had long vanished.

Along a 20-mile front, the Allies had advanced a

THE BATTLE OF CAMBRAI 1917. This was the scene of the world's first massed tank attack. On 20 December, the 434 vehicles of Brigadier-General Elles' Tank Corps, supported by an inadequate number of infantry and 40,000 cavalry, rolled over the Hindenburg Line west of Cambrai in an attempt to break the cycle of trench warfare. By mid-morning they had routed the Germans on a six-mile front, and Cambrai was open for the taking. Indecisive leadership resulted in the cavalry failing to capitalise on the breakthrough. By 30 November, many tanks had broken down; the Germans counter-attacked with a hail of poison gas shells, and the British had to withdraw from the salient they had created. They suffered 40,000 killed and wounded; the Germans lost a similar amount. A year later, Allied success in the Cambrai area, and the influx of American forces, began the startling series of victories that led to the German capitulation.

maximum of seven miles, at a cost of of 418,000 British and 195,000 French casualties; the Germans lost 650,000 killed or wounded. The machine-gun had mechanised killing, and for the "Pals" there was no more romantic talk of warfare.

Chapter Three

The Battle of Britain

In April 1940, Hitler launched his Blitzkrieg. Denmark and Norway fell rapidly. On 10 May, the Germans descended on the Low Countries. Belgium withstood the advance for 19 days, Holland for a fortnight. Simultaneously, 44 German divisions swept through the Ardennes in the Sedan area and converged on the Channel coast ten days later. The French Army was cut in two and the British forces were deprived of their supply lines. The British were 50 miles from the sea, with the German armour threatening them from the south and the Franco-Belgian front in the north collapsing. That the British managed to withdraw to the coast and form a bridge-head was remarkable. At Dunkirk, outnumbered, outgunned and surrounded, they fought a defensive action which enabled a third of a million men to escape across the waters.

The Italians declared war. After 37 days, France surrendered. In less than 11 weeks, Hitler had overrun most of Western Europe. Britain stood alone, on the eve of a battle which was to be fought high above the burning cities and the green fields of England.

As a precursor to Operation Sealion, the invasion of England, Goering, commander of the Luftwaffe, promised Hitler that he would bomb England into the ground. Analysis of German records after the war showed that Goering committed 1,480 bombers, 989 fighters and 140 reconnaissance aircraft to the attack and that he could draw on the resources of the Second and Third German airfleets, which possessed a total of 2,830 aircraft.

Battles

Against this vast aerial armada, Britain could only muster 666 combat-ready fighters. There were a further 513 in various states of repair at maintenance units. These comprised 55 squadrons. Initially the majority of the British aircraft were Hurricanes – only one-fifth were Spitfires. Some of the squadrons were Blenheim night-fighters or the old Defiants; they were little match for the superb German Messerschmitt 109 fighter. Lord Beaverbrook, put in charge of aircraft production, managed to increase output massively, and Air Vice-Marshal Sir Hugh Dowding had by September 59 squadrons.

The British had the advantage of radar and their advance knowledge of the enemy's approach proved crucial. The Germans had also developed an experimental form of radar, but so preoccupied were they with offensive operations that they failed to develop it further. Obsessed with the dive-bomber, the Germans never developed a long-range tactical bomber. Impressive though their force of Heinkels, Stukas and Messerschmitts was, it was not the force with which to bomb a nation into submission. Victory for the Germans depended on the success of the fighter arm of the Luftwaffe. The Blitzkrieg had given the German fighter pilots little opportunity to show their skills, since the majority of the Polish and French air forces had been destroyed on the ground; now they had to cut a swathe through the RAF so that the vast, droning formations of German bombers could pound Britain.

The first phase of the Battle of Britain began on 10 July. The Germans attacked Channel convoys and ports along the south coast of England, as a prelude to a German naval blockade which would include the mining of all south coast harbours. It was not a great success. The Luftwaffe suggested attacking the battleship *Repulse*, then in dry-dock. But Hitler, desperate to avoid a prolonged conflict with Britain, had made another peace offer – until the deadline expired on 19 July, he was adamant that no bombs should be dropped on British soil.

The twin-engined Ju-88 was employed in the attacks on shipping, but it was not available in sufficient numbers. The Ju-87, the Stuka, which had provided the impetus for the German Blitzkrieg, was easy meat for the Spitfires. Because of its externally hung bombs, the Stuka only reached 150 mph in its dive; the British would wait until the formation of Stukas broke up to attack, and then swoop on the sluggish bombers. The German Command continued to use it to attack convoys, and, much to the fury of the Messerschmitt pilots, blamed the heavy losses on the incompetence of the accompanying 109s. By 24 August, the targets had become the fighter airfields in the south of England. At first, to compensate for the limited range of their bombers, the Germans flew large groups of 109s intended to draw the RAF off the ground and into operational range.

The German fighter squadrons based on the Channel coast went into almost continuous action, flying two or three sorties a day over England. After take-off they would assemble in the coastal area and cross the English coast at a height of 21,000 to 24,000 feet. The trip took about half an hour at the narrowest point of the coastline. The 109s had a tactical flying time of only 80 minutes; they had about 20 minutes in which to conduct operations over England. Squadrons based in the Pas de Calais or the Contentin peninsula were even more restricted. By sheer dexterity the RAF pilots could prolong a dogfight until the Germans ran out of fuel.

Sometimes these large formations of 109s would be accompanied by one or two bombers, which the Germans called "decoy ducks". But the British quickly became wise to the tactic; the German fighters were of no importance, and the RAF conserved their resources to attack the bomber

Battles

formations. The German hopes of luring the British into large-scale combat were not realised.

Frustrated, the German Command ordered the 109s to attempt low-level strafing raids on airfields. The Germans found these well protected by anti-aircraft weapons, and rarely saw the aircraft on the ground, so well were they camouflaged. They also encountered a novel air defence: aerial cables, which were launched by rocket during a German attack and slowly descended by parachute. Initially the British flew in close formation, which made them very vulnerable to German ambushes. They quickly learned to adopt German tactics, and fly in a wide formation: small groups flew at different altitudes, so that each covered the other, and each pilot was able to look for the enemy rather than concentrate on keeping formation.

The German pilots appreciated the quality and courage of their opponents. The RAF were burdened with the inferior equipment. The 109 was a superb, fast fighter, whose armament and ammunition were better than anything the British possessed. The Hawker Hurricane compared badly in terms of speed and rate of climb. The British engines, fitted with orthodox carburettors, tended to conk out through lack of acceleration at critical moments; the 109s were fuel-injected. The Spitfires were different. Though 10 or 15 mph slower than the 109, they could perform steeper and tighter turns, making them superb defensive aircraft. Frustrated by their lack of range, and day by day depleted in number, the German fighter pilots slowly lost morale.

When the German fighters failed to achieve air-supremacy, Goering ordered bombing raids on British airfields. Few southern airfields escaped punishment, yet most continued to operate. Generally, too few bombs were dropped on the runways to inflict permanent damage, and the airfields were patched up overnight. German vanity

THE BATTLE OF THE ATLANTIC 1940–41. The great four-year struggle to keep open Britain's supply routes from America, upon which it was utterly dependent. It cost the lives of 30,248 merchant seamen, and 51,578 Royal Naval personnel. By the summer of 1941, Britain and its Allies had lost over 1,200 ships, and imports had fallen by a third. It was the work of U-Boats. Although the Allies sank 31, the Germans soon had 100 new submarines in the Atlantic. In 1942 U-Boats sank 1,160 ships and almost brought Britain to its knees. But the introduction of "Asdic" underwater detection, radar and new escort systems reduced losses and began to make inroads into the submarine fleet Though the Germans had 250 U-Boats operating in 1943, 67 of them were sunk between March and May, and Admiral Dönitz was forced to recall them to rest and repair. By the time they returned to the attack, Allied merchant production was exceeding its decreasing losses. Morale was further raised when the Royal Navy sank the German battle cruiser *Scharnhorst*, which had ravaged merchant shipping. By the end of 1944, the battle was won, though the U-Boat commanders struggled on until the end, then scuttled 221 of their surviving craft.

frequently ensured that all airfields that had been hit were crossed off the list of operational targets. Their pilots also claimed absurd numbers of kills. One German recounts that "it came about, one day, that according to the calculations in Berlin there were no more British fighters".

Battles

Pilots were in action up to five or six times a day. The mental and physical strain was enormous. The diminishing band of airmen emerged from their aircraft, reported on the previous sortie and climbed back into their cockpits. One Hurricane pilot landed, and remained so immobile in his cockpit that the ground crew rushed forward expecting to find him dead; he was asleep at the controls. In combat, some pilots were so tired they simply ploughed into the enemy formations.

Shortage of trained aircrew became a greater problem than shortage of aircraft. The numbers had to be made up by disbanding Army Co-operation squadrons and pitching into the fray pilots with little or no experience of flying high-speed attack aircraft. No front line aeroplanes could be spared for them to train on, and they had to learn on the job; there was more than one such novice who died on the same day he reported for duty. More than a third of all aircrew who took part in the battle had been little more than "part-time aviators" before the outbreak of the war.

For most RAF squadrons, each encounter with the enemy quickly became a frenzied dogfight, a dozen individual battles; they were too outnumbered to attack repeatedly in formation. Consequently, they would arrive home individually, with a couple of minutes between each aircraft. Sometimes, when one did not reappear, the pilot would telephone to say he'd been shot up and was at another airfield or had landed in a field. At other times, the telephone call would come from a rescue squad, detailing the number of the crashed and burned-out aircraft they had found. Another name would be crossed off. Few felt overwhelmed by emotion; there was no time for it.

Those pilots who survived continued to chop and change tactics. Their greatest fear was being caught from above. They would take off and climb to 15,000 feet before they even set out on the interception course given them by the controller. As they moved towards the incoming Germans, they continued to climb all the time, ensuring that they were above the enemy when they encountered him, and able to make the most of the one squadron attack their limited numbers permitted. Since the Spitfires were agile, particularly in the climb, by far the most effective assault on bombers was the frontal. Attacking in a line astern, the Spitfires would swoop, firing at point-blank range and pulling steeply up and away at the last possible moment. The British pilots would also attack from beneath, trying to rip open the unprotected underbelly of the bombers; a rear attack would bust up the formations, but exposed the fighters to rear-gun turrets.

The German Me 109 pilots were uncomfortable with their escorting role, in which they were restricted to flying in formation. Large formations simply meant that a pilot gave less of his attention to looking out for the enemy. The escorting role should have been filled by the Me 110, which had a longer range. But these proved largely helpless when matched against Spitfires, and could only escape by forming defensive circles. Again and again the 109s had to rescue the 110s; the latter were finally taken out of service altogether.

As the German losses of men and aircraft rose, Goering visited the Channel airfields, chastising the German pilots he believed were failing to protect the bombers adequately. One Luftwaffe officer, the young Group Commodore Adolf Galland, told him that he did not believe the Me 109 was suited to such escort activity; it was an attack aircraft. After a heated dispute, Goering asked Galland what one thing he desired. "I should like an outfit of Spitfires," he replied.

Goering's decision, on 7 September, to switch from bombing the airfields to attacking London in strength was a huge tactical error. The RAF's resources had been stretched

A defence post at an aerodrome

to their uttermost. Though British civilians now suffered dreadfully (in the first three months of the Blitz 12,696 Londoners were killed), the RAF were given time in which to patch up runways and reorganise depleted squadrons.

On the afternoon of 7 September 1940, 1,000 German aircraft assembled over the Channel coastline and began to move towards London. There were to be 38 large-scale raids on the city. The vast formations of bombers frequently failed to rendezvous with their fighter escorts who would afterwards latch onto an already escorted raid. Hence some formations flew with double protection, while others had none whatsoever – and were picked off by the RAF. The Germans believed that, by this point, the RAF possessed only 200 front line aircraft; yet they still inflicted heavy losses, and so decimated the Stuka formations that the plane was withdrawn from use in the raids.

The Germans did not possess aircraft capable of delivering large amounts of high explosive. They dropped an average of 500 tons of bombs per raid; when the Allies began to bomb Germany, their long-range Lancasters and Flying Fortresses were able to saturate the German cities, dropping bombs up to 10 tons in weight. The German bombing effectiveness was further reduced by the concentrated AA fire from 2,000 mobile guns, and the barrage balloons around London, which forced the bomber formations ever higher.

The climax came on 15 September. A colossal stack of German bombers, some twenty storeys high, droned in over the coast. 60 of them were shot down. Goering switched to night-raids, with an average number of 200 bombers. On 15 October, London was showered with 380 tons of high explosive and 70,000 incendiary devices. Though night-bombing continued intermittently into 1941, the raids had suffered astonishing losses, and on 12 October, Hitler had called off Sealion. The Luftwaffe

Battles

campaign against Britain ended in the Nazis' first defeat. It had cost the Germans 1,733 aircraft (the RAF claimed 2,698 kills). The RAF lost 915 aircraft and 481 pilots killed, wounded or missing.

Chapter Four

Stalingrad

A fter the Germans were held and turned back outside the gates of Moscow, Hitler determined to launch another major offensive in the summer of 1942, as soon as the Russian ground was hard enough to support the weight of his Panzers, and ordered another 800,000 men to the Russian front. Army Group North was ordered to take Leningrad; the Central Front was to hold its ground. In the south the Germans intended to break through to the Volga and the Caucasus and seize the oilfields. Ideology apart, Russia was invaded for its natural resources. Germany's resources and wealth had been stretched to the limits in the process of militarisation. The whole war was being fought by combustion engines, and Germany now had only what it produced synthetically or brought from the Rumanian and Hungarian oilfields. The Caucasus produced three-quarters of Russia's oil.

In June, Army Group South moved to take the Crimea and then cross the Kerch straits into the Caucasus. A typical Panzer pincer movement gobbled up the city of Voronezh further north, then swung south to enter the Caucasus and provide a strong flank against the Russian forces at Stalingrad.

Stalingrad had once been known as Tsaritsyn, the "Tsarina's city". It had been renamed Stalingrad in remembrance of an heroic charge that Stalin claimed to have led against the White Guard in 1918. An important trading-post for hundreds of years, it stood at the gateway to the Caucasus and the great eastern interior of the Soviet Union.

Battles

Apart from its strategic significance, it was of huge symbolic importance to Hitler, Stalin and the whole Russian nation.

With a population of around 445,000, Stalingrad was twenty miles long, but only three miles wide. It spread along the high western bank of the River Volga; there was a very small extension of the city on the east bank. At the northern end of the city were several industrial complexes of major importance to the Russian war effort: the Dzerhezinsky tractor plant, the Barrikadi gun factory and Krasnii Oktyabr iron and steel plant.

The Russians at Sebastopol proved tougher than expected, but otherwise the Germans proceeded according to plan. Voronezh fell on 6 July, and the main drive on the Caucasus and Stalingrad began. Russian counter-attacks were generally unsuccessful; they suffered heavily, and were routed at Kharkov, with the Germans taking a quarter of a million prisoners.

But Hitler behaved with customary immoderate haste. Instead of taking the Caucasus step by step, he ordered simultaneous assaults on the Caucasus and Stalingrad – though within weeks he had ordered the Fourth Panzer Army away from the main assault on the Caucasus and into the attack on Stalingrad. Colonel-General Friedrich Paulus – a clever, hard-working and conscientious German officer – had in the Sixth Army with which he attacked Stalingrad approximately 400,000 men.

Despite the reversal at Moscow, the Germans were accustomed to advancing rapidly through disorganised and badly equipped Russian forces. But, outside Stalingrad, the Russians were well-commanded and conducted the battle with astute tactics. Marshal Chuikov noted the co-ordination of the German air, artillery, armoured and infantry units in attack. He also noted the strict timetable of a German assault, and sought to disrupt this rhythm. The Russians evolved multiple lines of defence. In front of their main positions were reinforced outposts. The Germans customarily attacked at about 10 a.m. The Russian outposts would offer severe resistance, then rereat slowly towards their main divisions. The Germans, having lost the momentum of the assault, would discover that they had not yet faced the bulk of their opponents; they would pause to regroup, move the artillery forward and call back the aircraft for further strikes. By nightfall, they had rarely reached their objectives, and, dependent on co-ordinated attacks, would rarely fight at night. The Russians would then counter-attack.

Hitler ordered that Stalingrad be taken by 25 August. At high cost, and weakened by the transfer of artillery to reinforce the siege of Leningrad, Paulus had by 23 August entered the northern suburbs of the city. On that same day, the Luftwaffe launched one of the most devastating air raids of the war, killing 40,000 and wounding another 150,000, turning Stalingrad into an inferno. By the beginning of September there was not a leaf left on a tree in the vicinity of the city. By 2 September, the recalled Fourth Panzer Army had secured the territory west of Stalingrad and joined with Paulus to move on the centre of the burning city. Their assault left the 45,000 Russian troops clinging onto a few narrow bridge-heads along the banks of the Volga.

Chuikov saw that the main German tactic was the pincer movement, the operation of which was dependent upon the infantry being preceded by tanks, and the tanks by aircraft bombardment. To break this sequence, he ordered the Russian troops to get as close as possible to the German forces, so that aircraft and artillery could not shell or bomb the Russian positions. He ordered frequent, sudden attacks, and concentrated mortar barrages. The German troops, he believed, were less confident when bereft of their tank, artillery and air support.

Battles

On 13 and 14 September, the Germans poured towards the city centre, in an attempt to reach the Volga and split Chuikov's 62nd Army in half. By forming makeshift divisions, the Russians managed to hold the centre of Stalingrad against repeated German attacks. Control of the train station and the strategically vital Mamayev Hill flowed back and forth; such places could be taken and re-taken four or five times in the course of a day. Snow had begun to fall on the shattered city, vast acres of which now consisted only of standing chimney pots, since the wooden houses had long been burned. As the city turned white, the snow on Mamayev Hill remained black with the oil and filth of fighting. The hill was to remain the scene of ferocious combat until January the following year.

With his depleted forces drastically outnumbered, Chuikov had to adapt again. He ordered small groups of soldiers to infiltrate and take strongpoints throughout the city centre, to break the German advance. "What was needed", he wrote, "was for us to act so that every house in which we had even one soldier became a fortress against the enemy." To break up the German advance, the Russians drew them into street fighting to sap their mental and physical resources. The Germans had no time to regroup and launch organised counter-attacks. Chuikov split up the remaining Russian formations into small tactical units of commandos.

"The Germans call Stalingrad the Russian Verdun," said a BBC reporter. "But Verdun was a fortress; Stalingrad is an open city . . . this is not a battle for a locality or a river, but for street crossings and houses. Poland was conquered in 28 days; in 28 days in Stalingrad, the Germans took several houses. France was defeated in 38 days; in Stalingrad it took the Germans 38 days to advance from one side of the street to the other . . ."

The shipbuilding works continued to be able to repair the

THE BATTLE OF MOSCOW 1941–42. By
6 October 1941, the impetus of the German
Blitzkrieg had taken them to within 50 miles of
Moscow; by mid-October, they had encircled the
city, and 2 million inhabitants had been evacuated.
With winter coming, the Germans pressed for the
kill, but deep mud and Russian resistance slowed
their tanks down. They became embroiled in a
siege at Tula, 100 miles to the south, but took
Istra, a mere 15 miles from Moscow, on 22
November. Their 4th Infantry came within sight of
the city, but was halted by armed workers' units.
Meanwhile, the weather had turned bitterly cold,
for which the Germans were ill-equipped. They
were halted on 5 December, and thrown back by a
counter-attack launched by 100 Russian divisions,
who took dreadful casualties in the process of
repulsing the Germans between 100 and 200 miles
around the city. In the winter fighting, the Germans
lost up to 192,000 killed and wounded; the
Russians, probably twice that figure.

depleted Russian tank-force, and a local power plant
produced enough electricity to enable essential communications to be maintained. Even so, the Soviets' position was
precarious, and Chuikov had a desperate task to organise
his scattered forces.

In early September, a desperate attempt by Russian
reinforcements to break through the encircling German
Armies nearly succeeded when 10 Russian tanks almost
made it to the city; but the Germans closed around them,
and they were consigned to the flames. A trickle of

reinforcements reached the city from the east bank of the Volga, ferried across under remorseless air-assault (it was not uncommon for half a unit to be lost in such journeys). In November the river froze, and the supplies and soldiers began to move across the ice; the Russians were just holding onto a thin strip of territory on the river banks to the south of the city, on Mamayev Hill, and a few isolated pockets elsewhere.

Much of the fiercest fighting had taken place around the "workers' villages" and the Dzerhezinsky tractor plant. The workers there had been formed into a militia, and when the Germans reached the plant at the beginning of October they encountered strong resistance. The plant was shelled into a mangled wreck. There was no roof, no walls; it was a forest of girders twisting into the sky. But this steel jungle offered endless cover for the workers, among whom was one of the most celebrated of Russian women defenders, Olga Kovalova. The plant fell on 18 October. General Gurtiv's Siberian Division, holding the Red October factory, were subject to 100 assaults in the course of a single month.

The most famed pocket of resistance was a much-shelled apartment block, facing Solechnaya Street. On 28 September, Sergeant Jacob Pavlov and three others assaulted the house with hand grenades, expelling the incumbent Germans. In the basement of the house they found several badly wounded Russians still holding out. "Pavlov's House" became a boundary fortification, and a symbol of resistance. The handful of men defended the outpost for 58 days, against infantry, artillery and tank assaults.

Stalingrad brought about a change in the attitude of the Russian soldiers. At the beginning of the war they had been courageous, but naive in the face of German fire power. Then they had cultivated a nationalistic contempt of death, flinging themselves on the Germans without consideration

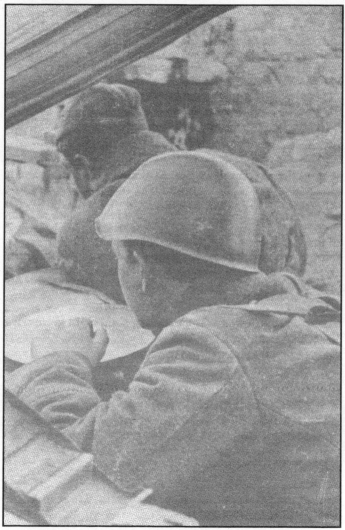

Machine-gunners on the outskirts of Stalingrad

for their lives. But, gradually, the Russians learned to fight with more circumspection; the function of the soldier was not to die valiantly, but to destroy the enemy and survive.

In late September a three-pronged Russian counter-offensive, with three armies and a force of a million men, cut the Germans off to the north and south of the city. On 19 November, a major assault began. The Russian Armies of Generals Vatutin and Yeremenko routed the Germans' Rumanian allies in the north of the city, and a mixed German and Rumanian force to the south. The armies met on 22 November. By the next day, the encirclement was completed; 300,000 Germans and their allies were trapped.

The push on the Caucasus had ground to a halt. But at Hitler's express order, the Germans in Stalingrad fought on, hopelessly, through the bleak winter. In December, a desperate attempt by Manstein's Army almost succeeded in reaching Paulus; but Hitler would not let the 6th Army pull out. Paulus rejected an offer of surrender at the beginning of January, but on 10 January the Russians bombarded the Germans with fire from 7,000 guns and mortars and split their army into parts. Within days they had taken the last German airfield and locked the enemy into a piece of territory only nine miles by fifteen.

Colonel-General Paulus and his staff were surrounded at their headquarters, located in the basement of a ruined department store. On 31 January 1943, Paulus received the glad news that Hitler had promoted him to Field Marshal. No German officer of that rank had ever been captured; it was tantamount to an order to commit suicide. That same day, Paulus and his staff surrendered. The German 11th Panzer Corps, holed up in the Dzerhezinsky tractor plant, held out for another two days.

Over 90,000 German troops were taken prisoner at Stalingrad. Among them were 24 generals. The Russians also claimed to have captured 1,500 tanks, 750 aircraft, 8,000 guns and mortars, and 61,000 other vehicles. Nearly 200,000 Germans died; the number of Russian casualties is impossible to ascertain. Recently, it was revealed that they may have been as high as one million. But the loss of manpower – an entire army – crippled Germany, and her forces were no longer perceived as invincible. Stalingrad was the turning point of the ground war; from then on, Hitler was lost.

Chapter Five

El Alamein

The turning point of the whole vast struggle
Field Marshal Erwin Rommel

The Second World War spilled over into North Africa because of the territorial ambitions of Hitler's ally, Mussolini. Italy was already the unloved overlord of Libya, wrested from the Ottoman Empire in 1912, and with the outbreak of hostilities in 1939 Mussolini sought to extend his new Roman Empire into Egypt. This was not only a British protectorate, it was the home of the strategically vital Suez Canal and the doorway to oil-rich Arabia. It was vital for Britain that she retained control of her Egyptian demesne.

The Italians had two armies in Libya, the Tenth and the Fifth, totalling about 200,000 men. On 13 September 1940 135,000 men of the Tenth Army, commanded by the distinctly unenthusiastic Marshal Rodolfo Graziani, rolled out of Libya into Egypt, where 60 miles in, at Sidi Barrani, they stopped to build camps and forts. Three months later, on 9 December, the British "Western Desert Force" under General Richard O'Connor (wearing the Silver Star for valour awarded him for fighting alongside the Italians in World War I) launched a surprise raid on the incompetent outposts at Sidi Barrani. The subsequent counter-offensive rolled Graziani back 400 miles to Beda Fomm.

And so was set the pattern of war in the desert. An offensive (and retreat by the other side) along the single coastal road, with the pursuer attempting to hook around the pursued to cut off the retreat whilst also striking at his defended positions (essentially the ports of Tobruk, Gazala, Benghazi, El Agheila, Tripoli). The war in the desert would likely have been over – in Britain's favour – by spring 1941 had not Hitler sent Mussolini a knight in shining tank armour: Erwin Rommel.

Born in 1891, Rommel had first distinguished himself in the First World War, winning a Pour le Merité in the Alpine campaign. Although he would be subsequently airbrushed as a "good German", he was an early sympathiser of the Nazi Party, and commanded the Führer's escort battalion from 1938 to 1940. During the invasion of France, he had commanded the 7th Panzer Division with such great distinction that he was the obvious candidate to command the German forces in the desert, which consisted initially of 5th Light and 15th Panzer Divisions. Although Rommel only arrived in North Africa on 12 February 1941 and knew nothing of desert warfare, he was a natural-born master of mobile operations – hence his admiring nickname, "The Desert Fox" – and by 24 March was on the offensive. After unceremoniously ejecting the British from Beda Fomm he went westwards at lightning speed. In a letter to his wife on 2 April 1941 Rommel mentioned that he expected a degree of consternation among his superiors at his decision to attack against all orders and instructions. His spirits were high, however, as he confidently expected that the attack would be a tremendous success, with booty and casualties continuing to favour the German Army, bringing in a spectacular victory that would convince his superiors that his plan had been sound. According to his letter, he was unable to sleep for happiness.

By 11 April Rommel was almost at the start line of O'Connor's December 1940 offensive. Tobruk, garrisoned by the 9th Australian Division, was surrounded inside the German-Italian gains.

However, Rommel's advance had severely extended his lines of supply from Tripoli, where the port was anyway being badly disrupted by British air, surface and submarine attacks. The British Navy, on the other hand, was doing a remarkably good job of getting supplies through to Egypt, including a convoy of tanks. Suitably armoured, the Commander-in-Chief Middle East, Sir Archibald Wavell, determined to launch a counter-offensive against Rommel.

Operation Battleaxe was a dismal failure, chiefly because the British tanks were picked off by the Germans' outstanding 88-mm guns, which, in the desert, enjoyed uninterrupted fields of fire. Their ranks thinned, the British tanks were then mercilessly preyed upon by Rommel's Panzers. Wavell was ignominiously dismissed, to be replaced by Claude Auchinleck from the army in India.

Operation Crusader, as Auchinleck's winter offensive was code-named, began on 18 November with nearly 700 tanks against 400 German-Italian tanks. Not the least objective of Crusader was the relief of the Allied garrison at Tobruk. A first attempt to reach Tobruk was rebuffed by the Afrika Korps, but on 10 December the Eighth Army (as the Western Desert Force had been newly christened) reached the port.

Defeat at Tobruk caused Rommel to retreat to El Agheila. But only until 21 January 1942 when he launched the familiar counter-offensive, and pushed the British halfway back through Cyrenaica to the Gazala-Bir Hacheim line. Both sides were now severely depleted of able men and armour; the British had lost 18,000 during Crusader, the Italo-German Army 38,000 men, while the British had lost 440 tanks, the enemy 340. Over the spring both sides refitted and resupplied. Under considerable pressure from Churchill Auchinleck planned a new offensive – but

Battles

Rommel struck first, launching the Gazala battle on 27 May, personally leading his tanks into the British positions. Two weeks later Auchinleck withdrew eastwards from the Gazala "cauldron" to a stronger position at Alam Halfa, near the railway halt of El Alamein, where the Qattara depression comes in close to the coast.

Behind him, Auchinleck had left Tobruk as a garrisoned "thorn" in Rommel's rear. Unfortunately, the 2nd South African Division resisted Rommel's siege for a single week only. The news was brought to Churchill in Washington, where he was conferring with Roosevelt. "I did not hide my shock from the President," Churchill later wrote. "Defeat is one thing; disgrace is another." Roosevelt, however, was supportive, and diverted 300 Sherman tanks – a worthy match, at last, for the awesome Panzer IV – to the Western Desert. Throughout the summer, the war of supply turned conclusively in Britain's favour. Desperate for a victory that would give Britain standing among her Allies, Churchill also purged the Middle East staff. Auchinleck was dismissed – an happenstance Churchill likened to "shooting a magnificent stag" – to be succeeded by General Harold Alexander; General Bernard Montgomery was brought in as commander of the Eighth Army. Wiry, ascetic, given to Napoleonic utterances ("The morale of the soldier is the greatest single factor in war"; "No leader, however great, can long continue unless he wins victories. The battle decides all") and showmanship (that beret), "Monty" had what his predecessors in the desert had not: the killer instinct. In case anyone doubted his desire "to fight and kill" he ordered all withdrawal plans to be burned. Alexander's orders to Montgomery were straightforward: destroy Rommel and his army. In Montgomery's opinion, this was an achievable goal, the ease of which depended entirely on timing. Rommel was expected to attack soon: if the attack came immediately, the British soldiers would have a difficult time; if he came in a week, the battle should just about favour them, but if he held off for two weeks, then whatever Rommel tried, he would fall before an unstoppable enemy. Montgomery was proud of his soldiers: they were seasoned veterans with excellent fighting experience. But they were bewildered and depressed at the recent setbacks, and morale was falling dangerously. Montgomery realised that they needed a victory, a clear, unarguable triumph over Rommel, with as few casualties to the Eighth Army as possible. The first such battle was not long in coming.

With the war of the stockpile going against him, Rommel had little option but to launch an offensive against the British line at Alam Halfa before materiel matters became worse. His plan was to launch a feint to the north, a holding attack in the centre, and throw the main attack at the southern end of the Alam Halfa line. This was to be undertaken by his elite Afrika Korps, consisting of the 15th and 21st Panzer Divisions, together with the German 90th Light Division and the Italian XXth Mobile Corps.

Rommel's plan was entirely expected; with the means and topography at his disposal there was little else he could do. On 31 August Rommel inaugurated the brief but bitter battle of Alam Halfa. It proved to be a serious mistake: Montgomery had anticipated the design of his attack, and taken steps to frustrate it. One of Rommel's forces was pushed up against Montgomery's New Zealand Division to the east, and found itself unable to move. Ground troops fired on them from all directions and the Desert Air Force fired on them from above. This action lasted for days, with Rommel losing tanks and soft-skinned vehicles at an alarming rate. When, finally, the air force sent Wellington planes behind his attack to bomb Tobruk, Rommel's last hope of re-supplying his forces was destroyed. Outmatched and penned in by the army and air force's deadly collaboration, he was forced to retreat.

Montgomery's confidence in his plan was such that he himself slept through much of this battle. A comrade of his swore that he woke Montgomery to tell him the news, to which Montgomery merely replied, "Excellent, couldn't be better", and went back to sleep until breakfast the next morning. (Montgomery himself had no memory of this incident, but was willing to accept that it had happened.) However, he was in at the death: seeing that Rommel's forces were struggling, he ordered the New Zealand Division area to close off their exits. Seeing this, Rommel's men were forced to retreat quickly through the only place left to them – the minefield from whence they had originally come. Montgomery left them there and called off the battle.

Aside from the sheer predictability of his plan, Rommel's design was undone by the poor quality of the Italian tanks (which had both an alarming tendency to "brew up" when hit and to break down in the midst of action), as well as the indisposition of Rommel himself who, through sickness, was confined to his truck. This was a crucial factor in the battle's failure for, as Desmond Young has observed, Rommel "relied much more on his personal observation and judgement during the progress of a battle than on a preconceived plan".

By the end of the battle of Alam Halfa on 7 September, Rommel had lost 3,000 men killed or wounded, and 50 tanks; British losses were 1,640 killed and wounded, and 68 tanks.

"With the failure of this offensive," Rommel recalled, "our last chance of gaining the Suez Canal had gone." A lull now descended on Egypt, during which Montgomery retrained his men for offensive action, and Rommel, uncharacteristically, deployed for defence, essentially at his original Alam Halfa position. Aside from the continued lack of petrol reaching him across the Mediterranean, due to sinkings by Allied ships, submarines and aircraft, Rommel was also dismayed by his own health, particularly a persistent stomach malady.

A month later, 22 September, Rommel was invalided to Germany, and Georg Stumme, a Panzer commander from the Russian campaign, arrived in North Africa as his replacement. On 24 October Rommel was telephoned by Hitler and informed that the British had launched a massive attack at El Alamein the previous day. Hitler asked Rommel if he would return to Africa. Despite his ill health, Rommel agreed to do so. The next evening he arrived at Panzer Army Africa HQ to find the battle of El Alamein in full rage, and the Italo-German front buckling dangerously under the Eighth Army assault.

For the attack at El Alamein Montgomery had conceived an offensive strategy markedly different from that of his predecessors, who had always sought a mobile war against the enemy. Montgomery understood, where they had not, that even the 7th Armoured Division lacked the chutzpah of Rommel's Panzers. To fight the Germans in their own "Blitzkrieg" style was nonsensical; what was needed was to force the Germans into a massive set-piece battle in which they would be annihilated. A "dogfight" Montgomery termed it. Accordingly, the main assault at El Alamein was by mixed infantry-artillery units of XXX Corps, and struck at the northern sector with the intention of "punching" two holes in the enemy's line, after which X Corps (comprising 1st and 10th Armoured Divisions) would pass through towards the coastal road and cut off the bulk of the enemy forces to the south. A diversionary attack in the southern sector of the front was intended to pin down the enemy, particularly the 21st Panzer Division.

The battle of El Alamein began on 23 October at 9.40 p.m.

El Alamein, infantry moving forward

under a brilliant moon. The entire artillery of the Eighth Army – nearly a thousand guns – opened fire on the enemy simultaneously. After twenty minutes of this, the infantry advanced: within three hours, they had captured the enemy forward defences on the XXXth Corps front without enduring many losses of their own. A half-hour halt was called to reorganise; at 1.30 a.m., the advance was resumed. Four hours of bitter fighting followed. At the end of that time, the Australian forces had accomplished most of their final objective, and the New Zealanders had secured all of theirs. The 51st Division in the north was not so successful: they were still 1,500 yards from their final destination, while the 1st South African Division in the south struggled for several more hours.

Meanwhile, the Xth Corps, who had begun their attack at 2 a.m. from the south, were suffering delays: the engineers working behind the artillery were held up lifting mines. It was not until 6.30 that the southern corridor was finally cleared. Once it was, though, the 9th and 10th Armoured Divisions moved forward along it, gaining a good footing on the eastern slope of the Miteiriya ridge before being stopped by heavy fire from the enemy. This hold-up combined with setbacks suffered by the 2nd Armoured Brigade and the 1st Armoured Division, whose corridor in the north was impeded with mines and artillery fire to such an extent that it was not until the 1st Armoured Division and the 51st Division joined forces to drive forward that the corridor was finally established at 3 p.m. These delays put the timetable back and made a break-out on the 24th impossible.

On the southern sector, however, the British feint achieved such limited success that Montgomery ordered Lieutenant-General Sir Brian Horrocks of XIII Corps to halt the attack and launch instead "crumbling" operations – local attacks of attrition. Even these proved costly, and

Battles

Montgomery altered the game plan to increase the weight of the offensive in the north. Simultaneously, the 1st Armoured Division was ordered to move westwards to Kidney Ridge (or Hill 28 as the Germans called it), where Rommel brought forward the 90th Light Division, and elements of the 90th Light, 15th Panzer and Littorio Divisions, as well as a battalion of Bersaglieri. The heaviest fighting of the entire battle ensued. Rommel made desperate attempts to attack Kidney Ridge, sending up his 90th Light Division and the Kampfstaffel, but they were outnumbered by the endless influx of fresh British forces Montgomery kept feeding into the attack. Perceiving that the British were aiming to win through to the area between El Daba and Sidi Abd el Rahman, Rommel moved the Trieste to the east of El Daba.

Meanwhile, the German and Italian dive-bomber formations attempted to break up the British lorry columns that were heading to the north-west – an effort that Rommel would later call "self-immolating". Sixty British fighters, far faster than Rommel's heavy bombers, pounced. The Italian pilots were forced to jettison their bombs over their own lines. The Germans fared a little better, but suffered massive losses as hundreds of British tracer shells blazed a criss-crossed inferno across the sky.

By afternoon, repeated British attacks to the south of Kidney Ridge succeeded in wiping out the battered 164th Infantry: 160 tanks penetrated Rommel's line to the south-west, coming close to breaking out before a violent attack from the remaining German and Italian tanks managed to force them back. There were not many tanks left to use against the British, though: already the 15th Panzer Division had lost 61 tanks, and the Littorio had lost 56 – tanks not merely incapacitated, but totally destroyed.

German troops were losing heart. The RAF were sending

formations of eighteen to twenty bombers over them at hourly intervals, with considerable casualties. It was beginning to feel like a battle they could not win.

By 26 October, it was clear to Montgomery that the attack was losing momentum in the key breakthrough areas, and he decided to regroup (a manoeuvre that caused Churchill to fear the battle was lost). Meanwhile, Rommel, seeing that Horrocks was only engaging in diversions, committed 21st Panzer northwards, although he knew it had no petrol for a return trip if needed. Now that Rommel had committed his reserves, Montgomery ground down the Axis Armies in a week of bitter attrition warfare on the northern sector of the front until on the 29th, Montgomery saw his opportunity to deal the telling blow. In the morning, the German 90th Light Division was moved to the coast road opposite the 9th Australian Division. To pin the 90th down, Montgomery ordered the Australians to attack the following night. Meanwhile, the 2nd New Zealand Division was ordered to force a gap (6,000 yards deep on a 4,000-yard front) a little to the south of the Australians and just north of Kidney Ridge. Once the hole had been made Xth Corps with the 1st, 7th, and 10th Armoured Divisions was to pass through it into open desert. Montgomery reported to General Sir Alan Brooke that after eight days' hard fighting in this minefield, the initiative had remained Montgomery's throughout and Rommel's counter-attacks had been managed without difficulty, leaving him ready for a hard blow that would topple him altogether. This planned attack was to go ahead that night; if it succeeded, it would destroy Rommel's army. Montgomery code-named the operation "Supercharge". It was unleashed at 1 a.m. on 2 November after a ferocious artillery bombardment, reinforced by bomber raids.

The corridor was successfully cleared, but when the 9th Armoured Brigade tried to pass through it was met with a veritable hail of anti-tank fire. Only 19 of the 94 tanks the brigade started with reached open country. But Rommel's dam had sprung a leak. Both sides raced their armour to the gap, and a furious two-hour tank-versus-tank encounter took place at Tel el Aqqaqir. Further south 15th Panzer was obliged to hold off the 10th Armoured Division as it nosed forward. The Axis forces fought valiantly and just managed to patch the leak. But in doing so they had suffered irreplaceable losses. By dusk 21st Panzer and 15th Panzer were down to 35 serviceable tanks. The Littorio Division had disintegrated. Only a few hundred tons of shells were left.

Rommel was under no illusions; the battle was lost. It only remained to retreat to a defensible position on the Fuka line. Hitler, however, refused Rommel's request to retreat, insisting that Rommel show his troops "no other road than that to victory or death".

To protest the order Rommel sent his ADC Berndt to see Hitler personally, but in the meantime felt he had no option but to follow the Führer's injunction. "I forced myself to this action," Rommel wrote, "as I had always demanded unconditional obedience from others, and consequently, wished to apply the same principle to myself." Accordingly, Rommel committed the last ounces of his strength to the battle. It was to no avail. Montgomery, aware of Rommel's every move by virtue of Bletchley Cipher School's cracking of the German Enigma code, merely focused his attack south of the German reinforcements. At nightfall on 3 November, Montgomery ordered the 51st Division and a brigade of the 4th Indian Division to move forward on a four-mile front and prise a hole through which the three armoured divisions could roll. In the early morning of the 4th, the breakthrough came. At 2 a.m., Montgomery directed two hard blows at the "hinges" of the final breakout area – and these two blows finished the battle. The armoured car regiments and divisions made it through into the open desert as dawn was coming up – a desert blessedly free of mines, where they could manoeuvre against the retreating columns of the enemy. From the other side of the hill, Rommel saw the small and inefficient tanks of XXth Corps struggling amidst enormous dust-clouds against 100 British heavy tanks. The Italians fought bravely, but nothing could save them: tank after tank was destroyed while the British bombarded the infantry and artillery.

By dusk the unfortunate XXth Italian Corps had disintegrated, and the Afrika Korps split asunder. The Korps commander had even been captured. General von Thoma sent away his lieutenant with his radio transmitter, telling the soldier that he didn't need it any more, as all the tanks and anti-tank guns had been destroyed. His comrade General Fritz Bayerlain, meeting with this lieutenant, went to investigate the whereabouts of his commander, and found himself an eyewitness to his downfall. What he encountered was a nightmare of fire. Armour-piercing shot whistled all around, and nothing was in sight but burning tanks and smashed flak guns. For a moment, it seemed as if there was no living soul present – and then through the haze, Bayerlain saw von Thoma, standing tall beside a burning tank, ignoring the hail of bullets. British Sherman tanks, on their way to Tel el Mampsra, had halted in a wide circle, surrounding the general. After a moment's pause, a Bren carrier headed towards von Thoma, who stood still holding his canvas bag in his hand, while a hundred and fifty vehicles flooded over Tel el Mampsra.

Despite his reluctance to counter the Führer's stand-fast order, Rommel had no choice but to authorise a retreat if he was to save anything of his army. In any case, some units were already in a headlong rush along the coast road back towards Tripoli.

As John Keegan has observed, "Montgomery has been reproved by post-war critics for an alleged failure to harry

Panzer Army Africa to its destruction in the days and weeks after El Alamein." Certainly, Montgomery exhibited caution after Rommel's pull-out on the night 4–5, and spent much of the next day regrouping, instead of chasing Rommel's tail. But Montgomery had already achieved his objective: a clear-cut win over the enemy. To have spent weeks fighting a running battle along the coast road would have muddied the result. Instead he kept up an organised pursuit that, by 23 January 1943, had Rommel back in Tripoli.

Besides, by any measure the Panzerarmee Afrika was destroyed at El Alamein. It had a mere 80 tanks left in working order.

Churchill later wrote: "Before Alamein we never had a victory. After Alamein we never had a defeat."

He was scarcely exaggerating. Like Stalingrad and Midway, Alamein was one of the battles that turned the fortunes of World War II.

Chapter Six

War in the Pacific

When the Second World War erupted, Imperial Japan was torn as to its desires. Its strategy had for decades been based on defensive principles. A rapidly expanding army and strong navy were oriented towards repelling the Soviet attack feared since the Russian revolution of 1917.

But a nationalist movement within the army – the "Imperial Way" – called for Japanese control of continental East Asia, partly for defensive purposes but also to replace the European colonists with a Japanese hegemony. The Imperial Way, operating without the authorisation of the government, moved the army to occupy Manchuria and the Korean peninsula, to block any imperialist Russian moves. But, to their frustration, they became bogged down in a prolonged struggle within Northern China and Manchuria, in which the Chinese Communists and Nationalists would periodically ally themselves against the Japanese invaders. When the war came to Europe, Japan, again moved by the Imperial Way, took advantage of the fall of France to occupy French Indo-China, from which they could establish airbases and mount an air and naval blockade of China.

The Americans feared rising Japanese nationalism, and the fall of France convinced them that they must develop a two-ocean navy with which to hold both the Atlantic and the Pacific. But such a course of action required time. They tried to keep the Japanese at bay through diplomacy, economic sanctions and aid to the British in Burma and the Chinese Nationalists. They then cut off oil and raw material exports to Japan and froze its assets, while increasing the amount of assistance that reached China in the form of "volunteer" airmen and their aircraft.

Japan had allied itself with Germany against Russia. It had elaborate plans to fight the Soviet Union, but had not considered a war with the Americans and British. When Hitler invaded Russia, the Imperial Way urged the seizure of Russia's resource-rich eastern provinces before the Germans took them.

The Imperial Navy, however, wanted a role in the wider conflict and argued for a "southern strategy", which would bring it into conflict with the Western Powers. Without American oil and British rubber, they argued, no assault on Russia would be possible. The Japanese should first take the Dutch East Indies and Malaya, ensuring adequate raw materials and cutting Allied supply lines to China. Then the Japanese Army could spearhead an attack on Russia. Unless the Japanese defeated the Americans in the Pacific, they would continue to arm the Chinese.

The Imperial Army reluctantly agreed to the navy's demands, among which was the invasion of the American Philippines. The Japanese Premier, Prince Konoye, was distressed by the prospect of such a war, and within the navy there were dissenters who opposed conflict with America, knowing that its industrial strength would defeat Japan. Konoye was persuaded to stand down in favour of General Hideki Tojo, the most influential officer in Japan. The Tojo regime declared the United States its principal enemy on 15 November 1941. They would create an outer defensive ring across the Pacific, conclude war in China, transform Manchuria into an industrial complex to equip the 2-million-strong Japanese army and seize Russia's eastern provinces (Hitler would smash the Russian Army); Britain and America would accept a settlement which recognised Japan's control over East Asia.

In November, the Imperial Fleet, under the command of

Isoroku Yamamoto, sidled out of Japan towards Pearl Harbor, Hawaii, where the Americans had based their fleet to deter the Japanese from any designs they might have on the Philippines. Yamamoto, who had been an opponent of the war with America, had concluded that Japanese hopes lay with a sneak attack which would begin – and end – the war at one blow, destroying the American Fleet at anchor; the Allies would then have few naval or air forces with which to oppose the Japanese drive on the Philippines, Malaya, Burma and the East Indies. He would do it all with six aircraft carriers, bearing a force of 360 aeroplanes.

Even as they steamed towards Hawaii, news came that Hitler had been stopped before the gates of Moscow; Japanese imperial ambitions were already dead on the ground. But, in their hearts, even the more sober of the Japanese leaders had long wanted this show-down with America.

The Japanese crossed the North Pacific in absolute secrecy, maintaining radio silence. The carriers came into position 200 miles north-west of Pearl Harbor before dawn on Sunday, 7 December, 1941. Escorted by superb Zero fighters, the torpedo planes and bombers screamed in, completely undetected, upon the exposed airstrips and battleships. When the three-hour attack was over, the Japanese had sunk four battleships, damaged four, sunk and damaged numerous other vessels, destroyed 250 aircraft and caused 3,500 casualties. The only fleet capable of opposing them in South-East Asia was sunk, though they had failed to find any American carriers.

With the Americans reeling – Japan had not even declared war – Japanese expeditionary forces thrust into Thailand, Burma, Malaya, Hong Kong, the Philippines, the Dutch East Indies and the islands of the South and Central Pacific, carrying all before them.

Battles

The Japanese 25th Army landed on the Malay peninsula and drove the British forces of Lieutenant-General A. E. Percival back on to Singapore. The great fortress of Singapore, of which Britain was so inordinately proud, fell after the Japanese seized the city's reservoirs. Though he outnumbered the Japanese, Percival had no option but to surrender, and his 70,000 men marched off into captivity on 15 February 1942. The loss of Singapore was a disaster for Britain; shown to be incapable of defending its Asian colonies, its prestige never recovered.

By the end of April 1942, the Japanese had driven the British, Americans and their Chinese Nationalist allies from Burma, back into its northern mountains, India and China. The Americans in the Philippines left all their B-17 Flying Fortresses out on the tarmac for hours after the Pearl Harbor attack, and were decimated. Without air defence Manila fell easily, though General MacArthur's forces retreated to the Battan peninsula and dug in grimly, holding off the Japanese for months. When the Japanese took their positions they exacted awful revenge. Within weeks a third of the 70,000 American and Filipino soldiers were dead.

The small British garrison on Hong Kong held out just two weeks. The East Indies fell in an offensive that lasted from December to February. The Dutch tried to hold Java. Rear-Admiral Karel Doorman – with five cruisers and a number of destroyers of Dutch, British, American and Australian origin – met the Japanese Navy at the battle of the Java Sea on 27 February. The Allies were routed, and Doorman chose to go down in the Dutch cruiser *De Ruyter*. The Dutch surrendered the Indies on 9 March. In April the Japanese bombed British facilities in Colombo, sank two cruisers and the aircraft carrier *Hermes*, and forced the British to withdraw to East Africa ports. The Japanese were now the uncontested masters of South-East Asia.

The US appointed Admiral Ernest J. King Commander-in-Chief of the United States Fleet; Admiral Chester Nimitz took over the shattered Pacific Fleet. King wanted action. Nimitz launched unrestricted submarine warfare against Japanese shipping, and the US deployed six of its still-surviving carriers in the Pacific to execute hit-and-run raids while the resources for some kind of Allied offensive could be mustered. The carriers conducted air attacks on Japanese positions in the Gilbert and Marshall Islands and New Guinea. The intense submarine war that the Americans waged over the next four years targeted not only military vessels, but merchant convoys; the nature of the Japanese attack on Pearl Harbor dispelled any qualms. Japan started the Pacific war with nearly 6 million tons of merchant shipping – the third-biggest merchant fleet in the world. By the end of 1944, over 150 American submarines were cruising the coastal waters of Japan, and the nation's merchant shipping capacity had been reduced to 40% of its 1941 level. In addition, the submarines accounted for a substantial proportion of Japanese military vessels, not least the largest aircraft carrier of the war, the enormous 68,000-ton *Shirano*.

After Pearl Harbor, the Japanese Army and Navy fell into disagreement about the next move. Believing that the Allies would be unable to counter-attack until 1943, the army wanted to turn the newly conquered Pacific Islands into strongpoints; the navy wanted to extend the range of Japanese influence by taking Hawaii – or even Australia – depriving the Allies of forward staging posts. But the army, with the majority of its forces tied up in Manchuria, standing off from the Soviet Army and fighting the Chinese Nationalists and Mao Tse Tung's Communists in the north, did not have the manpower. A compromise was reached; the Japanese would take Midway in the Pacific, the Aleutian Islands in the North Pacific, and a string of other islands – Port Moresby, New Caledonia and Fiji – to sever

73

Battles

Raising the American flag at the top of Mount Suribachi

the lines of communications between America and Australia. The capture of Midway – 1,150 miles west-north-west of Hawaii – would provide a base for long-range "Betty" bombers to drive the American fleet back to the coast of California.

King's hit-and-run raids paid off. On 18 April 1942, American B-25 bombers, operating from a carrier, the *Hornet*, bombed Tokyo and then went on to crash-land in friendly Chinese Nationalist areas. The Japanese public were horrified; their commanders thought the planes had come from Midway Island, and hastened with their plans to capture it, in the course of which they were to over-extend themselves and suffer their first major reversal.

Thanks to code-breakers, Nimitz knew of the Japanese designs on Midway, and that the assault would be preceded by an attack on Port Moresby. Four carriers were dispatched to block the approach to Port Moresby. The Battle of the Coral Sea began on 1 May. The main Japanese expedition steamed towards Port Moresby; a secondary force landed in the southern Solomons. Planes from the *Yorktown* sank several ships in the secondary expedition, but the carrier *Shoho* eluded them and united with the main Japanese fleet, in which were the big carriers *Shohaku* and *Zuikaku* under Admiral Tagaki. The two fleets hunted for each other until 7 May. Then Japanese planes sank two American support vessels; dive-bombers and torpedo-planes from the *Lexington* sank the *Shoho*. The *Lexington* took direct hits which caused massive explosions and forced the Americans to scuttle her. The *Shohaku* was heavily damaged by American aircraft. Both sides broke off the battle, but it was a set-back for the Japanese. With one carrier crippled and half the aircraft from the *Zuikaku* lost, they called off the invasion of Port Moresby. The Americans returned to Midway.

Battles

Admiral Yamamoto devised a convoluted plan of attack on Midway. The Aleutians would be attacked to draw the American carriers into a fleet of submarines. A carrier-launched air strike would then neutralise air and ground defences. The Japanese would go ashore, and the carriers would then be free to confront the Americans returning from the Aleutians – if they had survived. Yamamoto deployed a force of four "flat-tops" – the *Soryu*, the *Hiryu*, the *Kaga* and *Akagi* – equipped with Zero fighters, Val dive-bombers and Kate torpedo-bombers; aircraft far superior to the Americans' ageing TBD torpedo-planes and SPD dive-bombers (the standard carrier fighter, the F4F Wildcat, though hardy, was not as nimble as the Zero). He also had six battleships and the new *Yamato*, the largest battleship in the world.

Nimitz put his ships to sea before the Japanese submarine pack arrived. He decided to ignore the Japanese diversion on the Aleutians and force them into a battle ahead of schedule. Nimitz had the carriers *Enterprise* and *Hornet*, and the recently repaired *Yorktown*, but no battleships. Knowing the vulnerability of his TBD planes, he loaded the carriers with F4F Wildcats. The *Enterprise* and *Hornet* under Admiral Spruance, went to sea on 28 May, and the *Yorktown*, under Admiral Fletcher, on 30 May. They met up north of Midway.

The Japanese fleet approached hidden by foul weather, and the diversionary attack on the Aleutians duly took place. But Yamamoto and Admiral Nagumo, his subordinate, were disconcerted to find that the Americans showed no interest in the attack; nor could the American carriers be seen anywhere. The Americans were also looking for the Japanese fleet, and found them on 4 June when a PBY sighted the main force 200 miles south-west of the *Enterprise* and *Hornet*. Anticipating that the Japanese would be proceeding to assault Midway before they had located the American carriers, Nimitz ordered all aircraft on Midway into the air.

The first wave of 100 Zeros decimated the American fighters, which were old Buffalos and a handful of Wildcats. The Japanese lost about a third of their aircraft to the island's batteries, but caused significant damage. The American bombers at Midway – B-17s, B-26s, Vindicators and TBFs – were slaughtered when they attacked the Japanese fleet, and failed to score a single hit. But they did have one effect. Nagumo became uncertain as to whether he should order his aircraft to carry anti-ship torpedoes and bombs in preparation for their eventual encounter with the American fleet, or conventional weapons for attacking the airfields. As he vacillated, and struggled to manoeuvre his fleet to recover his aircraft, the American carriers were sighted. Nagumo desperately ordered the weapons on the planes to be changed once more; it took valuable time, and the Japanese fleet did not disperse to avoid concentrated fire-power, but stayed bunched together.

Spruance had planned to attack at 9 a.m., but on a hunch brought forward the time of attack by two hours, just as the Japanese were at their most confused. He launched 116 planes – Wildcats, TBDs and SPDs – from the *Enterprise* and *Hornet*. The *Yorktown*'s aircraft took off soon after. The weather was bad, and when the aircraft arrived at the target area, they found the Japanese gone. The *Hornet*'s aircraft had to turn back and refuel; many ditched in the sea. The others blundered on through the cloud, losing contact with each other. Finally, TBDs from the *Enterprise* guessed correctly the Japanese position; they had withdrawn slightly. Followed by TBDs from the *Yorktown*, they flew low at the Japanese carriers. But they had lost their fighter escort, and were utterly destroyed by Zeros. More TBDs from the *Yorktown* suffered the same fate. The Americans lost nearly 40 aircraft, without scoring one torpedo hit.

Battles

Preoccupied with slaughtering the TBDs, the Japanese failed to notice the arrival of SPD dive-bombers accompanied by Wildcats. The dive-bombers came down at 70 degrees; their 1,000lb bombs caught the majority of the Japanese aircraft on deck, in the midst of refuelling and re-arming. Enormous explosions ripped through three of the four Japanese carriers. Within a few seconds, the striking power of the Japanese Navy was destroyed. Only the *Hiryu* escaped. Later that morning, strikes launched from the surviving carrier damaged the *Yorktown*, but the Japanese lost many aircraft. In the afternoon, while American submarines finished off the burning Japanese carriers, dive-bombers found the *Hiryu*, its planes once again on deck. When it sank the next morning, Admial Yamaguchi elected to sink with it.

Yamamoto cancelled his plans to attack Midway, and beat a hasty retreat. But two of his cruisers – the *Mohgami* and *Mikuma* – rammed each other. They then came under attack by American dive-bombers. The *Mikuma* was lost, and the *Mohgami* utterly crippled.

Victory at Midway came at a price: the annihilation of all three torpedo squadrons and most of their pilots. But the Japanese lost 234 aircraft and four carriers, losses they were hard-pressed to make up. New carriers and ships were already coming off the American production lines. The Japanese could not hope to maintain their grasp on the Pacific.

With their carrier force crippled, the Japanese sought to create an airstrip on Guadalcanal Island, from which they might attack the American shipping links to Australia and New Zealand, and disrupt any Allied build-up in the Pacific. The Americans decided that construction of the airstrip should be stopped. The need for intervention became more acute after the Japanese landed in New Guinea and began an overland assault on Port Moresby.

The Australians, under General MacArthur, fought desperately against insurmountable odds.

On 7 August 1942, the American assault force of three carriers – the *Saratoga, Enterprise* and *Wasp* – provided cover for an amphibious assault by the 1st Marine Division on Guadalcanal. They met little resistance, though some ferocious fighting took place on neighbouring islets.

The Japanese retaliated with air strikes and sent troops by destroyer from Rabaul, New Guinea, down the channel between the Solomon Islands. (So frequently was this route used, and with such speed, that the Americans dubbed it the "Tokyo Express".) The Americans managed to complete the Guadalcanal airstrip, known as Henderson Airfield, but the Japanese continued to press strongly.

By October the Americans were at crisis point, and had only two operational carriers left. The American commanders were tired and pessimistic. Nimitz brought in the aggressive Vice-Admiral Halsey. At Guadalcanal over 12 and 13 November, a vast "Tokyo Express" escorting 13,000 troops was confronted by five American cruisers and eight destroyers. Two American cruisers were lost, but aircraft from Henderson Airbase and the *Enterprise*, brought into the attack though damaged, sank a Japanese battleship, a cruiser and seven troop transports. On 14 November, the Americans lost two destroyers and a further two were rendered impotent, but the big guns of their cruisers sank the Japanese battleship *Kirishima* and a destroyer. Only four Japanese troop transports survived. Over the succeeding weeks, the Japanese launched further "Tokyo Express" runs, and sank another two American cruisers. But the Americans managed to consolidate their position on the island. By the new year, there were over 40,000 troops waiting to repulse further Japanese attacks.

Frustrated, the Japanese constructed another airstrip on the island of New Munda, but they were forced to go on the defensive. Americans patrolling Guadalcanal, looking for Japanese troops, were amazed to find them gone; they had been evacuated – the tide was turning. By the end of January 1943, Australian and American troops had endured the horrors of jungle warfare to expel the Japanese from eastern New Guinea; Port Moresby was safe, and the Allies began to look at Japanese positions further north-west. While the two sides regrouped on ground and sea, a prolonged aerial battle was fought between the American aircraft located at Henderson and Port Moresby and the Japanese air force flying from Rabaul and its bases throughout the northern Solomons. Despite the superior quality of the Japanese Zero, the pilots were exhausted, and were being rapidly swallowed up by the blue waters of the Pacific. The Americans were careful to rotate their pilots to keep them fresh, and had much improved their tactics and equipment.

Attempts by the Japanese to reinforce central New Guinea were foiled at the battle of the Bismarck Sea, on 3 March 1943. A transport of 7,000 soldiers, protected by Zeros and eight destroyers, was attacked by 100 Allied aircraft, among which were B-25s and A-20s. Expecting the usual, ineffective medium-level bombing, the Japanese were surprised to see the planes flying at wave height and skipping their bombs across the water into the sides of the ships. Supported by marauding PT boats, the attacks continued for several days. The convoy was utterly ravaged. Twelve ships were sunk, 300 men lost and over 20 aircraft, at a cost of five American aircraft.

A massive attack on Guadalcanal by 300 Japanese aircraft was ineffective, as the pilots were by now so inexperienced. They exaggerated their success to Yamamoto, who planned a trip to congratulate them. It was, in all senses, a vain and foolish trip. Nimitz received intelligence of Yamamoto's journey, and on 18 April sixteen American P-38 Lightnings from Henderson ambushed the Admiral's aircraft and escorting fighters over his destination. Yamamoto went down in flames. The Japanese, bereft of skilled pilots, short of ships, their supply routes threatened and their manpower shrinking, had now lost their most competent officer.

With the bulk of Japanese land forces tied up in the prolonged struggle on the Chinese mainland and in Burma, Admiral King planned a strategy which was intended to cut off Japan from its army in Manchuria, and destroy its seaborne forces by forcing them to defend the Carolines and the Marianas. Japan would then be bombed into submission without the need to invade it. The Army Chief of Staff, George Marshall, wanted to invade Japan; but General MacArthur, apart from a wish to liberate the Philippines, was largely in accord.

By October the Americans, Australians and New Zealanders had made inroads into the Japanese position in the Solomons and eastern New Guinea, and threatened the Japanese stronghold in the northern Solomons. The Japanese began to reinforce by pulling troops out of Manchuria, but their supply routes and the base at Rabaul were endlessly harassed by aircraft, PT boats and submarines. There were new American carriers at sea, and air strikes were set in motion throughout the Central Pacific islands.

Industrial might was beginning to tell. Equipped with new ships, Vice-Admiral Spruance's newly created Central Pacific Fleet departed to assault the Gilbert Islands in early November 1943. It was part of a three-pronged attack by King, who knew that the Japanese could not deploy their forces to resist simultaneous attacks.

American Marines went ashore at Bougainville in the northern Solomons, from which they would be able to conduct air-operations against Rabaul. During the assault,

Battles

97 planes from two carriers attacked Rabaul and damaged six Japanese cruisers. A carrier-assault on Rabaul sank two destroyers and crippled a further cruiser. The Japanese pulled back their fleet. Then, after six days of air and sea bombardment, 100,000 Marines went ashore in the Gilbert Islands, led by the modestly entitled Major-General "Howlin' Mad" Smith. When the Gilberts had fallen, the Americans poured the Sixth Army and Marines ashore on New Britain. These landings, and the taking of the adjacent New Ireland, cut off the Japanese at Rabaul.

Despite the desire of some of his generals to launch a single strike westwards, King persisted with multiple attacks on the Japanese. MacArthur led a drive in the South-West Pacific, and Nimitz, in the Central Pacific, proceeded via the eastern Carolines, the Marianas and the western Carolines. They would meet at the coast of China.

Nimitz launched a dozen fast carriers, accompanied by a half-dozen escort carriers, assorted cruisers, battleships and destroyers, at the Japanese-occupied Marshall Islands at the end of January 1943. The ships and aircraft pounded the island of Kwajalein, then put ashore 40,000 Marines and Army under "Howlin' Mad" Smith. The Japanese, reinforced by their excellent troops from Manchuria, resisted fanatically, making night-time suicide charges; 8,000 died, among whom many chose to commit mass hara-kiri rather than face the dishonour of surrender.

Within days, the Marines were landing on Eniwetok; simultaneously the planes of Task Force 58 launched a vast attack on the Japanese stronghold on Truk, intending to finish off their fleet. The ships were gone, but the Americans destroyed 250 Zeros and sank a quarter of a million tons of merchant shipping. The American aircraft went onwards, over the heads of their navy and armed forces, to the Marianas, where Corsairs and Hellcats shot down 74 Zeros and sank 45,000 tons of shipping.

Nimitz decided to by-pass the isolated strongholds of Truk and Rabaul; these posed no major threat. The next objective would be to secure Saipan, Guam and Tinian in the Marianas; these could then be used to mount long-range bombing raids on the Japanese homeland, and as forward bases for the proposed invasion of Formosa and the Chinese mainland.

With American submarines wreaking havoc, the Japanese were suffering acute shortages of raw materials. Stocks of fuel were so low that on some occasions potato alcohol was used as a substitute for aviation fuel, and new pilots were denied training flights. Increasingly, the Japanese would rely upon the men of their forces to perform acts of suicide to defend the Imperial homeland.

Stunned by the speed of the American advance, Emperor Hirohito appointed General Tojo, already Premier and Minister for War, to Chief of the Army General Staff. He located the Combined Fleet at Palau in the western Carolines and began to pull back Pacific-based 18th Army forces along the New Guinea coast, to consolidate at Aitape and Hollandia, out of reach of American bombers. But the Americans outflanked them. On 22 April MacArthur's forces landed at Hollandia and Aitape, which they subdued in two days of heavy fighting; the Americans had now cut off the 50,000 Japanese troops of the 18th Army.

The Japanese Navy moved 650 planes and nine carriers, carrying a further 450 planes, to defend the Marianas. MacArthur assaulted the New Guinea island of Wakde, and within days the Americans were ashore on Biak. The prospect of losing this strategically vital island frightened the Japanese; they decided to attack MacArthur immediately. Instead of using their air force in concentration, they lost nerve and sent only 200, with ground forces to follow. The Japanese were decimated by malaria and American firepower, and the convoy of ground forces was turned back. The Japanese tried again, this time sending an escort that included the staggering *Yamato* and *Musashi* – 72,000 tons apiece, the biggest battleships in the world. Before they were anywhere near their objective, Nimitz pounced on the Marianas. As a prelude to the invasion, Task Force 58 – 1,000 aircraft from 15 carriers – attacked the airfields, destroying 200 planes. The survivors were sent to ChiChi Jima and Iwo Jima to regroup, and the *Yamato* group was ordered to link up with the Japanese Third Fleet in a hastily conceived attack on the approaching American Fifth Fleet.

The American Fifth Fleet was carrying the 127,000 troops of the 5th Amphibious towards the island of Saipan. Spruance knew that the Japanese Navy was approaching, but proceeded for the moment with the invasion. While aircraft bombed the defences and destroyed Japanese aircraft on Iwo Jima, the troops went ashore, on 15 June, against furious resistance from the 32,000 Japanese. While the battle raged on land, Spruance learned that the Japanese Navy was closing. He was worried that the Japanese would be coming in two groups, as they had at Midway, and was perhaps unduly cautious, choosing to wait rather than search and destroy. On the morning of 19 June the first of the Japanese aircraft – some 340 – left their carriers and hopped towards the island of Guam, where the Japanese planned to refuel their planes in order to wheedle two strikes out of each sortie. The Hellcats of Task Force 58 massacred the inexperienced Japanese pilots, who could do little other than fly in formation. Some 400 aircraft from the carriers and Guam were shot down, at a cost of 30 American aircraft. The Japanese carriers were left defence-less, and the Americans stalked them for hundreds of miles, with submarines and aircraft accounting for three.

The Japanese on Saipan resisted until 9 July. The defenders of Guam and Tinian were dead a month later. The surviving Japanese troops in New Guinea were abandoned, and forgotten about. Weeks later, they reappeared in the rear of the Sixth Army, and launched a fierce, though pointless, assault. It took a month to subdue them. Many simply disappeared into the jungle, to re-emerge months or even years later. By the end of October 1944, American B-29s were flying from the Marianas to bomb the Japanese mainland.

In the wake of the defeat in the Marianas, Tojo resigned. The new Japanese leaders drew a new defensive line: the Philippines, Formosa, Okinawa in the Ryukyu Islands, the Kuriles and their own homeland.

The four islands of the Philippines were the next American objectives: Luzon, Samar, Leyte and Mindano. In particular, they wanted to secure control of the waters off Luzon, which were bounded by Formosa to the north-east and Ahoy, on the coast of China, in the north. The Japanese reinforced the Philippines and their offshore islands.

The American carriers first attacked Palau Island, off Mindano, and attacked Mindano immediately afterwards. The minimal air-resistance convinced Rear-Admiral Halsey that Mindano should be by-passed, and they began bombing Leyte. Over the days that followed, the American aircraft destroyed hundreds of Japanese aircraft based on Leyte, Formosa, Okinawa and even the first of the Japanese islands themselves.

But the territory had to be taken by soldiers. The American ground troops who went ashore at Palau were caught unawares by new Japanese tactics. They had dug in back from the beach-head, evaded the bombardment, and now had to be winkled out with flame-throwers and napalm in weeks of bloody fighting.

The Japanese retaliated with their Victory plan, a suicidal attack by the Combined Fleet. Split into three elements, the fleet was to conduct a pincer movement on the American forces off Leyte, while a decoy force of denuded carriers drew away the protecting fast carriers. Meanwhile, the Kamikaze Corps on Luzon were to crash-dive into carriers and troop-transports. Over 23 and 24 October, the pincers were engaged by American submarines and aircraft, and the Japanese Southern group lost three cruisers; the Central group lost the enormous battleship *Musashi*. But, believing that these groups were retreating, the American carriers were lured north to attack the Japanese carriers; in addition, the six fast cruisers of the invasion fleet turned and pursued the Southern group.

Although the fast carriers destroyed the Japanese carriers and the cruisers sank two battleships and three destroyers, when dawn came neither the carriers nor the cruisers had returned. Bad communications, and too much presumption, had left the invasion fleet naked. The Central group crept back, and the helpless American fleet looked in horror at the distant bulk of the Japanese ships. Two destroyers and two escort carriers were sunk. With the fleet at their mercy, the Japanese, fearing that the fast carriers would soon return, made off. Their navy was finished.

Leyte was conquered by mid-December. At the beginning of February 1945, having subdued fanatical resistance in Manila, the Americans took the Philippines, and planned to invade the Japanese homeland by November.

The Japanese had lost the Pacific. Without air or sea forces, they now lost Burma; Australian and Dutch troops, supported by American ships and aircraft, liberated the East Indies. Japanese armies were cut off, by-passed and left to wither away in Thailand, Malaya and Singapore, Sumatra and Java.

Russia now promised to declare war on Japan after the defeat of Hitler. The Japanese had to bring troops from northern China into Manchuria, and found themselves on the defensive against the Chinese.

The Allies built up the Chinese Nationalist and Soviet forces while they roamed the air and sea largely at will, tightening their blockade of the home islands. Two targets remained before a full-scale invasion of Japan: Iwo Jima and Okinawa. Though they were already flying over Japan, their bombers were tried by the distance and, lacking the necessary fighter cover, had been afflicted with unacceptable losses. From Iwo and Okinawa islands, fighter escorts could accompany them, and they would be able to bomb industrial centres with impunity. Privately, many looked at the lack of success achieved by strategic bombing in Germany, and thought that they might have to kill the entire civilian population before capitulation. In March they made something of a start with the infamous fire-bombing of Tokyo, which killed 83,000 in one single night; it did not bring surrender.

The assault on Iwo Jima began on 10 February 1945, when 1,000 carrier aircraft sortied towards Tokyo to provide strategic cover for the Iwo Jima landing. After pounding the black volcanic island for three days, the Americans went ashore. They had no idea what they would encounter; the 23,000 garrison had burrowed deep under the sand and lava to form a chain of pillboxes and caves. Bogged down in the volcanic sand, the first American forces were cut down by withering fire from an enemy they could not see. Marines made it ashore and attacked the three airfields, while a regiment went up Mt Suribachi, using flame-throwers to kill the pockets of resistance. After three days, they raised the flag over the mountain. But it was not until the night of 2 March that the Japanese defenders exhausted themselves in a last suicide charge.

On 1 April, after air and sea bombardment, 180,000 troops, both army and Marines, began wading onto the six-mile-long island of Okinawa, where the Japanese 3rd Army had strategically withdrawn, offering no opposition before the Americans advanced into the interior. They counter-attacked by air and sea on 6 April. By the time organised Japanese resistance ended on 22 June, the Americans and their Allies had lost 12,000 dead, over 700 aircraft and 36 ships; the dead Japanese and native Okinawans numbered well in excess of 100,000. The Americans had little hope that an attack on the Japanese homeland could prevail without similar bloodshed; the Japanese still had 2 million troops held back.

Japan was defeated when Okinawa fell. But no word of surrender issued from Tokyo. While Chinese, American and Russian forces advanced on the continent, an escalating scale of bombardment was therefore planned. This would culminate in the dropping of the atomic bomb; if this final horror did not work, the Americans would reluctantly initiate Operation Olympic, the invasion of southern Japan.

On 6 August the "Enola Gay" dropped the A-bomb on Hiroshima; on 9 August Nagasaki suffered the same fate. With the Red Army swarming across Manchuria, and the rest of her cities burning, the Imperial will broke and the Japanese agreed to discuss surrender. The war cost the Japanese Army 1,130,000 dead, the Navy 300,000 and the civilian population 672,000.

Chapter Seven

Kursk

By June 1943, the Eastern Front extended for around 1,700 miles, from Finland to the Crimea. The Germans were severely stretched and had suffered terrible losses at Stalingrad; they would not be able to mount another attack of the size of those in 1941 and 1942. But the German generals knew that the Russians had suffered still more. By the end of 1941, nearly $3^1/_2$ million Russian soldiers had been taken prisoner by the Germans; 2 million of these were dead a year later, through hunger, cold, forced labour, disease and massacre. In the course of the war, the Russians lost over $8^1/_2$ million soldiers, and another 16 million were wounded. In addition, 19 million civilians died. Aware of the staggering scale of Russian losses, the German generals believed it was conceivable that the Russian forces could be worn down to such an extent that Germany might extricate its armies. The Germans now lacked the resources to hold the entire front, and had to look instead to corner a substantial portion of the Russian forces.

The rectangular Kursk salient seemed to offer such an opportunity. Formerly farming countryside, its brief occupation by the Germans had turned it into a wasteland. The Germans had withdrawn, and the salient was now filling up with Russian troops, posing a distinct danger to the Germans' Centre and South Army Groups. They could cripple the Russians, however, if they made a quick strike. Field Marshal Manstein presented this, among other offensive options, to Hitler. But since the other options involved giving ground, Hitler would only countenance attacking the Kursk salient. He gave orders for the operation, code-named Citadel, and instructed that the best armies, the best leaders and best weapons were to be employed in the "encirclement of the enemy forces deployed in the Kursk area".

These orders were issued on 11 April. But the officers who would execute the pincer movements – Colonel-General Model and Field Marshal Manstein – were having second thoughts about the ease with which the Russian defences might be penetrated. Furthermore, it was pointed out, Germany's tank strength was low; production of Panthers was not yet in full swing.

Hitler agonised and conferred. It was pointed out that the Russians not only expected the assault; they were counting on it, and had withdrawn their armoured divisions to the rear of the salient, waiting to pounce once the Germans had been exhausted by the defenders. In fact, the Russians, thanks to the efforts of British code-breakers, were aware of every hesitant step the Germans were taking towards the battle. Marshal Zhukov wanted the battle, and intended it to be fought on his own terms. The Germans would be worn down, their armour destroyed, and the Red Army would launch a counter-offensive. Defending the salient were 1.3 million men; and there were 150 guns per mile along the Germans' axis of advance. The Stavka – the Red Army Command – had brought together no less than 3,500 tanks and self-propelled guns; 2,000 waited in support of the defenders, and the remainder lurked in the rear with the Fifth Guards Army.

By late June, Hitler, preoccupied by trouble in the Mediterranean and the problematic development of his prized Panther, was still vacillating. His generals wanted Citadel cancelled. But Hitler was committed to the principle of offensive action; he dreaded the prospect of trench warfare, and argued Citadel was a way of shortening the

German front line and the best opportunity for a morale-boosting victory in the East. Privately, he confessed that his great plans for the East were now in ruins. But he set a date – 5 July – for the operation, and justified the attack as a necessary attempt to disrupt the Red Army's gathering force. Publicly optimistic, his generals returned to the front filled with foreboding.

On the north of the salient was Model's Ninth Army, extended along a front of 35 miles. Model had 14 infantry, six Panzer and two Panzer grenadier divisions. Seven of the infantry divisions were assigned to Citadel. Model's left flank to the east and north was protected by the Second Panzer Army. He could call on substantial air cover from Luftflotte 6.

On the south side of the salient, across a front of 28 miles, Manstein's main force was provided by the Fourth Panzer Army, under the command of Colonel-General Hermann Hoth. Under Hoth was the most powerful strike-force ever assembled by a German commander. It included nine of the finest divisions in the German Army. Including the forces on Hoth's flanks, Manstein had four Panzer grenadier, seven Panzer and 11 infantry divisions for Citadel, and could call on air support from units of Luftflotte 4.

The SS Panzer divisions had around 130 tanks and 35 assault guns apiece, and each had around 14 of the fearsome Tiger tanks. Each SS division also had six Panzer grenadier battalions apiece. But the most powerful of the armoured divisions at Kursk was the Grossdeutschland. It was equipped with 163 tanks and 35 assault guns; of these, 14 were Tigers and 104 were Panthers.

In conference with Manstein, Hitler had estimated that it would take 300–400 of the new Tigers and Panthers to break through at Kursk. But in the end, the southern forces had only a combined total of 205 of these. In the north, Model had only 30 Tigers. To compensate, he had 90 of the 60-ton Elefant tank-destroyers. The Panthers, on which so much depended, continued to be plagued with technical problems.

Around the Kursk salient the German Army had concentrated some 10,000 heavy guns and mortars, and nearly 2,400 assault guns and tanks. This represented over 70% of their total armoured strength on the Eastern Front, and an astonishing 46% of Germany's total front-line Panzer strength. Only 860 tanks remained along the rest of the Eastern Front.

The battlefield was a broad plain, broken up by numerous valleys, small copses, irregularly laid-out villages and sporadic rivers and brooks, some of which were swift-moving. The incline of the ground favoured the defenders, and the untended cornfields which covered the landscape made visibility difficult for tanks. There were few roads – only dirt tracks, which rain turned to mud.

Model and Manstein had developed different tactics with which to breach the Red Army's defences. Model planned to use infantry, combat engineers and artillery to make breaches in the Russian line into which he could then feed his tanks. Manstein, short on infantry but possessing superior armour, intended to use his Tigers to punch a hole in the defences, and then pour in his Panthers and Mark IVs; the infantry, armed with grenades and automatic weapons, would follow to soften the path for the mobile Panzer grenadiers. Momentum was of the essence in this plan; once the tanks were through, they were not to stop, not even to assist disabled vehicles and their crews. These orders were to bring about the death of many tank crews in the subsequent battle.

Alerted by their excellent intelligence network, the Russians were not deceived by the decoy operations; they knew that the Germans would attack between 3 and 5 July.

Adolf Hitler

Battles

Convoys of tanks and guns rumbled into position to fortify the already bristling front line.

Around 3 p.m., on 4 July, the German artillery and Nebelwerfers (rocket launchers) began a barrage. As the barrage climaxed, the hot sticky weather broke and a fearful thunderstorm began. Panzer grenadier units of Hoth's forces on the south of the salient advanced; their first objective was to secure the low hills in front of their lines, which would provide their artillery with a position from which to pulverise the Russian forces within the salient.

The violence of Hoth's attack took the Red Army by surprise. By 4.45 p.m. the German artillery observers were in the hills around the village of Butovo, left of the front's centre. Aware that this attack was the preface to the main offensive, the Russians bided their time; they had limited shell and rocket stocks, and knew that they would consume half of these in the counter-bombardment.

They let loose at 2.20 a.m. on 5 July. They had no clear idea of the locations of German forces, but the ferocious bombardment created widespread confusion and suppressed the German artillery. By 5.30 a.m. the Russians reported heavy infantry and tank attacks on both fronts of the salient. In the north, on central front, Model's initial infantry push was held up by minefields. Initial probing attacks were then held up by an artillery barrage, and it was not until 8.30 a.m., when he began to throw in his Mk-IVs, supported by Tigers and the lumbering Elefants, that the Russian defences were breached. This stab through the defences could not be turned into a mortal wound; Model was holding the tanks necessary for this in reserve. Mk-IVs began assaulting the Russian front line, at the junction of the Russian 15th and 81st Rifle Divisions. If these could be prised apart, the entire right wing of the 70th Army was threatened.

Rokossovsky had expected the Germans to head due

south, down a railway line on the eastern end of the battle line towards the village of Ponyri; he had held his forces back, so as to be able to strike back at the Germans when they reached that extremity, probably on the second day. Now he deduced that the main thrust of the attack was more to the west, towards the village of Olkhovatka. He rapidly re-deployed his tank corps, but then found that Ponyri was under assault from tanks and Panzer grenadiers.

But Model's attack started to unravel. The minefields were simply too thick. As fast as the Germans cleared paths, the Russians re-layed the minefields. Sometimes the Russians left paths through them, channelling the German tanks into a concentrated barrage of anti-tank fire. When the vehicles were knocked out, the accompanying troops had little protection from the machine-gun nests. Behind their front lines, the Russian troops frequently managed to separate the tanks from their accompanying infantry. The Germans found that many of the areas they believed they had taken possession of became fierce battlefields.

The Elefants became a burden. They were excellent defensive weapons, but hardly used to this swift offensive role. Once they had broken through the Russian lines they were morooned amid a maze of slit trenches; without machine-guns and bereft of smaller tanks to protect them, they became prey to the mobile Soviet infantry.

By the end of 5 July, Model had lost over 100 tanks and self-propelled guns, and suffered great casualties. The deep defences had broken up his attack force. Tanks must have infantry to protect them from assault by satchel-bombs, mines and flame-throwers; but many of Model's Tigers were scattered in isolated groups, without infantry. He also feared that his flank was not exposed to Russian counter-attacks from the Fifth Guards Tank Army.

In the south, on Hoth's front, the attack came at 3.30 a.m.,

THE BATTLE OF WHITE RUSSIA 1944. After Kursk, the Germans were reduced to about 3 million men along the Eastern Front; they faced nearly 6 million Russians. The next spring the Russians attacked across a 450-mile front with four armies – 189 divisions, with 31,000 guns, 5,200 tanks and self-propelled guns and 6,000 aircraft. A vast partisan army harassed the Germans in the rear and within a week the German front was broken in six places. Thereafter the Russians advanced 10–15 miles a day, taking the cities of Minsk, Pinsk, Vitebsk and Bobruisk in rapid succession. By mid-July 1944, the Soviet Armies were pushing the Germans back into Poland; in 36 days of continuous battle, they had destroyed 25 divisions and caused 350,000 casualties.

preceded by massive air strikes by a force of 800 Stukas, bombers and escorting fighters. Hoth's objective was to push north through the salient towards Kursk and link up with Model's Ninth Army. But such a route would bring him into direct confrontation with Katukov's First Tank Army. He also knew the strength of the Russian reserves and realised that such a passage would expose his flank to the Soviet Fifth Guards Tank Army, which was lurking to the east of the salient. He therefore decided to take a north-eastern passage, secure the strategically vital area around the village of Prokhorovka, and protect his flank from the Russian reserves before he moved on to Kursk. Hoth did not tell his headquarters his intentions; thus they were not intercepted and remained unknown to the Russian forces. His reticence was a stroke of genius.

The tanks of Grossdeutschland became bogged down by swamp and minefields. Mk-IVs and Mk-VI Panzers skirted the swamp and attacked the village of Cherlasskoye, five miles inside the Soviet front line. When the Russians finally retreated the village was a pile of rubble, littered with burned-out tanks, the twisted remains of guns and the inevitable charred and distorted bodies. The important village of Korovino was also taken.

Hoth's main battering rams were the Totenkopf, Leibstandarte and Das Reich divisions which constituted II SS Panzer Corp. This ideological flagship was a massive force, having 400 armed fighting vehicles, induding 42 Tigers and a Nebelwerfer brigade. Many of the battalions were led by flame-throwing brigades of SS Panzer grenadiers. At the village of Beresovka these took a terrible toll.

When night fell, the Germans had penetrated up to 12 miles in the south. The infantry of the assault battalions lay exhausted in slit trenches. The tank crews, who had become highly dependent on amphetamines, were unable to sleep; they lay paralysed, caught between their need for sleep and the constant state of alertness wrought by the drugs. Despite the ground taken, and small losses from enemy fire, they had still fallen short of their objectives.

In the north, on the central front, Rokossovsky launched a counter-attack on 6 July, throwing in three tank corps. But it foundered on formerly Russian minefields, which the Germans had reinforced, and the Russians instead took fixed positions to act as a breakwater against a renewed German assault.

In an effort to take high ground from which he could shell Kursk, Model was now compelled to send into the assault the forces he had retained for the push on Kursk once the breakthrough had been achieved. Three Panzer Divisions – the 2nd, 9th and 18th – moved forward to attack a front of 20 miles. Across a string of low-lying ridges at the heart of the defences on the central front, the Russians had amassed 3,000 guns and mortars, 5,000 machine-guns and over 1,000 tanks. As the encounter turned into an apocalyptic four-day tank battle, the Russians continued to pour in reinforcements. At the peak of the fray, 2,000 armoured vehicles fought for the high ground between the villages of Soborovka and Ponyri.

Led by the Tiger companies of Major Sauvant, the Germans ground forward yard by yard. But the Russian defences seemed endless. Everywhere the Tigers encountered dumps of dug-in T34s and suicidally courageous squads of Russian "tank-busters". The Germans continued to be plagued by mechanical failures, and by 7 July Sauvant's thrust was faltering.

On 8 July Model's armour made three thrusts into the centre of the Russian defences along central front: the villages of Teploye, Olkhovatka and Ponyri. At Teploye, the main objective was Hill 272. Time and again the Germans assaulted it, after attacks from swarms of Stukas who dropped 550lb bombs on the anti-tank positions. But the Russians were well dug-in and well camouflaged. They preferred to fight the Germans at close range, where their anti-tank rifles and dug-in T34s took a devastating toll. The Germans took the hill three times, but the Russians continued to recapture it.

The German attack also ground to a halt at Olkhovatka, and the battle around Ponyri was so bitter that it became known as the "Stalingrad of the Kursk salient". The Germans held the village, but could go no further. On the first day of Citadel, Model's Ninth Army had advanced five miles; over the following seven days it managed only a further six miles. As Zhukov had intended, the attack had been absorbed by the threefold line of Russian defences and stalled within tantalising distance of Kursk.

On 11 July the Russians began to launch a series of counter-attacks which the Germans repulsed with artillery and Nebelwerfer bombardments. The impetus was now with the Soviet forces; their aircraft began to attack the German tank formations from behind, aiming at the vulnerable armour on the rear of the vehicles.

In the south, the Russian front was in greater peril. General Vatutin had planned counter-attacks for the morning of 6 July, but had been persuaded instead to dig his tanks in, as Rokossovsky had done on the central front. Enormous tank battles followed. German Stukas screamed in to bomb and strafe, some equipped with experimental armour-piercing cannon, causing consternation among the Russian armour; in vain, the Russians utilised smoke shells in order to deceive the Germans into believing that their tanks were already on fire.

The SS battalions of the II SS Panzer Corps ground their way through the defences of the Russian Sixth Guards Army, impeded in some places by knee-high mud and swollen bridgeless streams. Totenkopf, on the right flank, advanced faster than the others, making some 20 miles. But the Russian artillery, anti-tank gunners and air force exacted a heavy price; between 6 and 7 July the German tank strength on the southern front declined from 865 to 621.

Sensing that the Germans were near exhaustion, the Stavka now began to move the immense Russian reserves, including the Fifth Guards Tank Army, to engage the Germans in a crushing counter-attack. The Fifth Guards Tank Army was to take up position north of the village of Prokhorovka. They had a long journey to make, in stinking heat. Mile after mile of sweaty soldiers poured over the fields of yellowing corn, enveloped in thick clouds of dust raised by an endless, rumbling column of tanks, self-propelled guns and artillery pieces towed by tractors.

The Germans continued to make intermittent progress on

the southern front. But the rapid movement of some elements exposed the flanks of other forces, and they were not able to roll back the Russian defences across a broad sector. The right flank of the SS Panzer Corps was left exposed by the slow advance of the forces of Army Detachment Kempf, and on the morning of 8 July, 60 T34s and a mighty wedge of supporting infantry emerged from woodland near the village of Belgorod in an attempt to cut the German supply lines. They were spotted by the Luftwaffe, and attacked by 64 bombers and fighter-bombers. Within an hour, 50 tanks were aflame, and the infantry had been decimated by fragmentation bombs.

On 9 July the SS divisions clawed and scratched their way across the barren, scorched soil and barbed wire of the final line of Russian defences in their sector. In the afternoon, a division from Totenkopf's 1st Panzer Grenadier Regiment forded the last natural obstacle to their advance, the River Psel. The objective now was to link up with the other advance elements of Hoth's IVth Panzer Army – including Grossdeutschland – and push north to Prokhorovka.

A passage through Prokhorovka was the last opportunity for the Germans to reach Kursk; the alternative was the passage through the heavily fortified Russian town of Oboyan to the north. In the east, Kempf's forces were now advancing rapidly. Between the corridor they had punched and Hoth's forces to the west was a vast concentration of Russian forces. If Hoth and Kempf could link up at Prokhorovka, they would also have a chance to surround and destroy the main Russian forces in the south of the salient.

Fifth Guards Tank Army, with 850 vehicles, was in position north-east of Prokhorovka on the morning of 11 July; it joined an immense body of infantry and other mechanised armour. The 24th Army, 4th Guards Tank Corps and 4th Mechanised Corps moved from the reserves to defend the city of Kursk against any breakthrough. The Germans now assembling around Prokhorovka did not know that the enormous Russian reserves were yards away.

Kempf's forces leapt forward over the defenders at the town of Rhavets on the River Donets. Placing a captured T34 at the head of his column of tanks, Colonel von Oppel-Bronikowski Bake drove right through the Russian defence without firing a shot. When Russian tanks eventually became curious, he personally destroyed two with sticky-bombs, and then made the river in a frantic final dash. By dawn, the Germans were across the Donets. German aircraft, thinking that only Russians were on the north bank, bombed them while they were holding a staff conference; 15 senior officers were killed and 39 wounded, including Oppel-Bronikowski Bake himself. Kempf remained tied down by the Russians until 13 July and never made it to Prokhorovka.

At 8.30 a.m. on 12 July the Russian artillery began to shell the woodland south of Prokhorovka where they believed the German tanks of the SS divisions were concealed. The tanks of the Russian 29th and 18th Corps stormed across the scorched wheatfields; at the same moment, the SS Panzer Divisions launched their own attack. The opposing tanks had no time to manoeuvre. The commanders on both sides lost control of their formations and abandoned any attempt to direct the free-for-all, rapidly obscured by thick clouds of smoke and a vast dust storm raised by the squealing treads of hundreds of tanks. In the metallic fracas, the monumental Tigers lost all their advantages of weaponry and armour. Soon the Russian T34s broke through and were running all over the German lines.

When night fell, both sides assumed defensive positions. Lightning flickered across a 20-mile front. The Germans had been blunted and turned, their last resources exended; they were now on the defensive. And as the battle began at Prokhorovka, the Russians launched a long-planned counter-attack against Model's stalled forces on central front.

When news of the Allied invasion of Sicily reached Hitler on 12 July, his attention – and hopes – began to wander from Citadel. On 13 July he told Manstein that the forces to repel the Allied thrust through Italy and the Balkans would have to be found from the Eastern Front; Citadel would have to be discontinued. The action continued for a few more days, but it was the prelude to the German retreat to the Dneiper. Within two months, the Germans would withdraw some 150 miles along a 650-mile front. By the end of July Hitler would demand the withdrawal of his depleted SS divisions.

Hitler tried to reason that Citadel had been a success, in that it must have depleted the Russian reserves sufficiently to prevent them mounting a winter offensive; but it was an unmitigated disaster, putting an end to what little hope had been left on the Eastern Front. Coming after the awful defeat at Stalingrad, the failure of the elite II SS Panzer Corps to break through at Kursk sapped their morale to breaking point. The Russians noted, with some satisfaction, that after 12 July the SS stopped committing their forces in the customary dense combat formations, sending only small reconnaissance groups of three or four tanks.

In the fighting at Prokhorovka they lost some 400 tanks; but 112 of these were soon patched up and back in action. Such was the scale of Soviet tank production that reinforcements constantly kept ahead of losses; within a fortnight of Citadel, they had nearly 3,000 tanks in the Kursk salient.

The Germans, by comparison, had few reserves left. Manstein's Fourth Panzer Army suffered 133,000 casualties in the course of July and August. He got 33,000 replacements. His advance of only 25 miles had cost over 300 tanks; many less than the Russians, but, given Germany's low tank output, these were irreplaceable. Throughout the whole of the Eastern Front, the Germans suffered 365,000 "irreplaceable" losses in the summer of 1943; most of these were at Kursk and the subsequent retreat.

Citadel had been undertaken in the knowledge that the attacking German forces were infinitely inferior in number, and that, had success been achieved, there were insufficient reserves to exploit it. The Germans had dismissed their enemy as lesser beings; but the Russians outfought and outthought them. Only an arrogant mind, in the first instance, could contemplate the possibility of conquering Russia's vastness; the defeat at Kursk was a consequence of that legendary German chauvinism.

Battles

THE WARSAW UPRISING 1944. An armoured division of the Soviet Army reached the suburbs of Warsaw on 31 July 1944. Believing that the Russians would be in the city within hours, Warsaw's 40,000-strong Underground Army responded to Radio Moscow's call for an uprising. Having food and weapons sufficient only for a week, they attacked the Germans with home-made bombs and small-arms. The SS retaliated with customary savagery, though they were hard pressed by the courageous Poles, who initially prevailed, but were then divided and cut to pieces by SS Panzer divisions and air attacks. Forced underground, the Poles fought bitter battles in the sewers of Warsaw. The Poles owed allegiance to their government in exile, and Stalin, having tricked them into fighting, now refused them aid, even forbidding the British and Americans to drop supplies. Without ammunition, the Poles were forced to surrender on 2 September. About 15,000 fighters and 20,000 civilians were killed or subsequently massacred. German casualties were 19,000, of which 10,000 were killed; in addition, another 7,000 were missing, possibly Russian turncoat troops who had taken the opportunity to flee. Hitler ordered Warsaw to be destroyed. When the Soviet forces deigned to enter it in January 1945, it was utterly ruined.

Chapter Seven

D-Day: Normandy 1944

An invasion of France had been on the Allied agenda since America had entered the war. As the American Navy dealt with the war against the Japanese, the Americans committed the bulk of their army – which would swell to 8 million men – to fighting Germany in Europe. The Americans continued to pursue the principle of an invasion. The British had deep reservations about it. The grounds for this equivocation was their dwindling manpower. The British population was ravaged by the war, and the intended invasion would require the deployment of Britain's last reserves of male strength, upon which a future hold on its crumbling empire depended. They feared that heavy casualties would inevitably be suffered by the inexperienced British forces under inexperienced officers – for the First World War had soaked up the blood of those who should have provided the officer backbone of the army.

In the event, Operation Overlord – the invasion of Normandy – was the most extraordinary logistical feat of modern warfare. The statistics are quite staggering. The invasion involved a total of nearly 3 million men on land, air and sea; 284 destroyers, cruisers and other combat vessels; over 10,000 vessels to transport and land the forces; and nearly 8,000 aircraft.

On 6 June preceded by airborne landings of varied success, this massive armada assaulted the Normandy coast between Quineviile and Cabourg, along five stretches of beach code-named Utah, Omaha, Gold, Juno and Sword.

Battles

By the time resistance crumbled in late August, the Germans had lost 450,000 men, of whom 240,000 were dead or wounded, 1,500 tanks, 3,500 guns and 20,000 vehicles. The Allies, who had throughout possessed overwhelming superiority in terms of quantities of military hardware, had been pushed to the limit. They had suffered 209,672 casualties, of whom roughly half were dead. In addition, 28,000 Allied airmen had perished over France.

Although the Germans had long been prepared for an invasion, they were uncertain where the blow would fall. Too much of their army was tied up on the Eastern Front, and though Rommel had wanted to move Panzer divisions held in reserve up to the Normandy coastline, Hitler had ordered that they remain inland. He was convinced – as were many others – that the Allied attack would fall at the Pas de Calais, or in southern France. The confusion among the German command provided the Allies with a priceless advantage, and was largely the result of a deception operation – "Fortitude" – which used everything from inflatable tanks to false radio transmissions to indicate the build-up of an invasion force intended for the Calais region. Though the British had no secret agents within the German command structure, they had been able to "turn" almost every German agent in Britain, and used them to send a stream of false information back to Berlin. A further source of intelligence were the "ultra" intercepts of coded German messages. Alan Turing and his team had cracked the Axis codes. Though the information could be erratic, it at least provided the Allies with advance warning of German movements, and enabled them to manipulate German anxieties.

The Allied forces that went ashore were divided into the American 1st Army, under Lieutenant-General Omar Bradley, and the British Second Army, under Lieutenant-General Sir Miles Dempsey. The entire army invasion force was known as 21 Army Group, and was under the direction of General Sir Bernard Montgomery, the hero of El Alamein. The American 1st Army was further divided into the US VII Corps, under General J. Lawton Collins (which assaulted Utah Beach), and the US V Corps, under Major-General L. T. Gerow (which assaulted Omaha Beach). The British Second Army comprised XXX Corps and I Corps. The former contained the 50th Infantry and the 8th Armoured, which had triumphed in Africa. It was commanded by Lieutenant-General Bucknall and landed at Gold Beach. The latter was under the command of Lieutenant-General J. T. Crocker, and landed at Juno and Sword Beaches.

Since the invasion had been postponed from the 5th, most of the soldiers had been aboard their ships for days. They emerged to climb down precipitous scrambling nets into their landing craft, and approached the grey coast, enshrouded by smoke from the bombing and naval barrage.

As the coast became clearer, German shells began to land among the approaching craft. The Allied barrage was lifted according to the set timetable of the invasion. But the congested conditions had resulted in many landing craft running behind schedule, and the delay between the barrage lifting and the troops hitting the beaches resulted in many Allied deaths. It was low tide, a source of frustration for the Germans, whose meagre coastal defences in some sectors had been ranged on Rommel's insistence to cover an Allied landing at high tide. When the landing craft stopped, the men would face a short wade through three feet of water to reach French soil.

Most of the first wave of invaders were accompanied by DD Sherman tanks, converted to be amphibious, so that they could rise out of the sea and begin firing on the defences. At Utah Beach, 28 of the 32 DDs made it to the shore and were instrumental in blasting away the few heavy guns of the defences. The VII Corps then realised that they had actually landed over a mile south of their intended beach. The Americans rapidly overwhelmed the lone defending regiment, and began to pour ashore in force. Later, as they tried to move inland, they discovered why the Germans had under-garrisoned the area; it backed onto heavily flooded, marshy plains, which made progress dreadfully slow. The crucial momentum of their push inland was lost. But 23,000 men came ashore at Utah, on the first day, at a cost of only 197 casualties.

Omaha, where two-thirds of the American forces were concentrated, possessed the strongest natural fortifications; hills and cliffs rose to 200 feet above the beach. It was also the most heavily defended area of the coast. The American plan for Omaha was wholesale frontal assault with overwhelming manpower, dependent on prior bombardment from sea and air to weaken the German defences, a scenario familiar to all those who had fought in the Great War. It failed, just as its forerunners did. In their desire to avoid bombing the invaders, the Allied aircraft had dumped most of their bombs too far inland to do much damage to the defences. The German bunkers and pillboxes had also been constructed to withstand gunfire from the sea, and the awesome naval barrage had little effect.

To compound the Americans' problems, a ten-knot wind whipped up the waves, drowning some of the infantry. In addition, due to a hideous error, 32 of the infantry's supporting DD tanks were launched 6,000 yards from the beach. All but five went to the bottom, drowning most of their crews. The attempt to land artillery also failed and the first wave of American infantry arrived without any armoured support.

The Germans brought all their guns to bear on the shoreline; shells and mortars began to cascade upon the invaders and every machine-gun along the Omaha sector traversed the sands. Within minutes, a thick flotsam of bodies and debris accumulated along the shoreline. The shattered hulks of beached landing craft and ruined equipment provided some cover for the troops, but they also blocked the beach-head, preventing further landings and utterly ruining the invasion timetable. Nearly half the 270 engineers who came ashore to blow the German defences were dead or wounded, and only six of the 16 armoured bulldozers had actually made it ashore; three of these were then destroyed. The wheels of the assault could not be halted; men and munitions piled in on top of the gathering residue of the previous wave. Tank units were losing 50% or more of their strength before they even reached the beach.

To complete the confusion, nearly every radio set on the beach was out of action. Back on the ships, no one had any idea what was happening; from offshore, the sight of milling landing craft, wrecked tanks and floundering bodies suggested that the attack had collapsed. The chaos spread to the landing vessels, which, jostling for position off the overcrowded beach, formed an enormous traffic jam. Some of the more inexperienced landing craft crews began to panic, dropping the men far from the shore and occasionally abandoning them altogether when the boats were hit.

Some units of Rangers gathered their shattered ranks, scaled the cliffs and destroyed German fortifications. Having secured their immediate objectives, they were then forced to halt, lacking sufficient forces to advance any further. Finally, amid the confusion, a few committed leaders and isolated bodies of troops made the breaches that would allow the American forces to burst out of the bottle.

By early afternoon, the Americans had overwhelmed the German defences, and were moving off the beach, into the surrounding countryside. In some places they were close to their D-Day objectives. Amid the narrow lanes and thick hedgerows – the bocage – they would encounter new difficulties.

The British and Canadians at Juno, Gold and Sword fared better than the Americans at Omaha. At Sword, the assault began at 7.25 a.m., an hour after the Omaha landing. The British landings were led by specially adapted tanks, the "funnies", which carried a variety of equipment. Most of the DD tanks despatched in the first wave to Sword also arrived safely. With the armour ashore and quickly engaging the local defences, the landing proceeded on schedule. Casualties were heavy for some units – particularly the Commandos – but overall the Sword landing was a great success.

On Juno beach, to the west of Sword, the Canadians had a harder baptism. Their landing was delayed, and the intervening shift in the tide resulted in the concealment of an offshore reef, on which many foundered, becoming entangled in the German beach obstacles of mines, barbed wire and steel tank-traps. Nearly all the first wave of 24 landing craft were stranded and some 90 landing craft were lost in total. Although most of the DD tanks made the shore, they arrived behind the troops, too late to stifle resistance. The troops were also supposed to receive artillery support from self-propelled guns mounted in the hulks of old Centaur tanks. The majority of these capsized their landing craft and ended up at the bottom of the sea; only six out of 40 reached the beach. The Canadians fought their way off the beach quite rapidly, but immediately encountered stiff resistance; some units took 50% casualties.

At Gold, the British 50th Division lost 46 members of 47 Commando when three of their five landing craft struck mines. The tanks arrived, again, too late to give the first wave of infantry supporting fire, and the 1st Hampshires and 1st Dorsets were accordingly mauled. The Centaurs, as at Juno, mostly went to the bottom of the sea. But they progressed inland quickly, against fierce opposition.

By 10.30 a.m., the British Second Army had put ashore 15 infantry battalions, seven Commandos, seven tank regiments and supporting units. The British had by far the most ambitious objectives. Montgomery had promised that they would move so rapidly from the beach-head with armoured thrusts, that they would envelop Caen on the first day.

When night fell, the Allies had fallen short of their objectives on all fronts. It was to be 10 July before the invaders were able to break out of Normandy. The Allies possessed overwhelming firepower, but the quality of the German armour – and their weapons generally – was better suited to the nature of the conflict. The Germans also made intelligent tactical use of the terrain.

The battle for Normandy was fought firstly on the exposed beaches, then inland, in swamp, open fields, orchards and the countryside of the bocage, with its narrow lanes and dense hedges. For the first two months, the Allies were rarely fighting across open countryside, in which their numbers and the air support they could command would be dominant. Contrary to many of their expectations, the troops found themselves engaged in ferocious, close-quarters encounters with well-established and concealed Germans. The cover provided by the woods – and particularly the hedges which prevented the passage of tanks – impeded rapid organised advances, and resulted in bottlenecks of Allied forces of vehicles and men. The Germans sallied out of their defensive positions to infiltrate the Allied lines, using the hedges to launch ambushes. It was the Americans who suffered worst in the bocage. They rarely saw their enemy, except when dead, but spent much of the time crawling forward under hedgerows or lying in

EL ALAMEIN 1942. In North Africa, on 23–24 October 1942, General Montgomery's Eighth Army of 200,000 men and 1,100 tanks, with commanding air support, attacked Field Marshal Rommel's Italians and Afrika corps of 96,000 men and 500 tanks. Minefields and artillery held up the advance, and after five days the British had lost 10,000 men without achieving a breakthrough. Told to triumph, whatever the cost, Montgomery launched a further attack, which, assisted by RAF assaults, broke the enemy line and exposed their flanks. By 3 November Rommel was in retreat. The Axis forces were then pursued 1,500 miles by the British forces, who drove them from North Africa. Axis casualties were anything up to 10,000 men, with 30,000 taken prisoner. It was Britain's first land victory of the war, and raised shattered national morale.

shallow ditches. Stationary, they were more vulnerable, but often American officers could not persuade their troops to stand up and move forward; if they did, at the next burst of gunfire – no matter how distant – they would fall flat again. In such encounters, the "panzerfaust', a disposable projectile launcher, was particularly effective.

In contrast, the Allied commanders showed a lack of imagination in pushing their forces, strung out in conventional formation, across the fields towards the waiting Germans. Allied advances were at first concerned with military precepts such as not exposing the flanks of an attack force to the enemy. Hence, a unit that punched through German defences would seek immediately to link with the units to its left and right, and would confront pockets of German resistance rather than simply by-passing them, cutting them off, and depriving them of reasons to fight further. Later the Allies adopted the tactics that the Germans used so successfully throughout their campaigns – to drive through the enemy with gathering momentum, and, having penetrated, to secure crossroads and communication links to the rear of the enemy forces.

The problem the hedgerows presented to the tanks and armour was partly solved, after weeks of frustrating losses, by the enterprise of an American army sergeant, who persuaded his commanders to fit steel "tusks" to the Sherman tanks. Known as "rhinos", these customised Shermans were able to batter their way through.

Much has been made of the differences between the Allied commanders. The Americans, who were providing the overwhelming bulk of the men and material for the invasion, resented the way that they were constantly expected to defer to "superior" British military skill in the command structure. Englishmen held all three subordinate command positions under Eisenhower, the Supreme Commander: Sir Bernard Montgomery on land, Sir Bertram Ramsey at sea, Sir Trafford Leigh Mallory in the air. Another Englishman, Air Chief Marshal Sir Arthur Tedder, served as Deputy Supreme Commander. A rift opened between Montgomery and the Americans, particularly Eisenhower. Montgomery was accused of being autocratic in preparation, and of promising results from his own British Second Army which it consistently failed to deliver. Furthermore, though one of the best military commanders of modern times, "Monty's" vanity led him to create revisionist versions of his plans, explaining away failure as complicated success (throughout the Normandy campaign he mounted costly attacks that, when stalled, he described as diversionary or attritional exercises). He later claimed sole responsibility for the conception and success of Overlord.

There were sour relationships between the services themselves. The Allied Air Forces, in particular, were highly resentful about being called away from the strategic bombing of Germany. "Bomber" Harris had somewhat peremptorily claimed that strategic bombing could bring Germany to its knees; there was no need for an invasion. The air forces of both Britain and America were attempting to establish their credentials as the decisive force in warfare. There was less opportunity to assert such an identity over the fields of Normandy. The low-level sorties in support of ground troops were hazardous; many pilots felt that they were being called upon to die in the execution of army responsibilities. The heavy concentrations of Allied infantry were vulnerable to friendly fire, particularly from wild bombing by American Fortresses.

But Overlord could not have succeeded without Allied domination of the air, and the working relationship between ground and air forces survived and was in some ways improved after the Americans established direct radio links between their forward units and their supporting aircraft, enabling them to call down fire with greater accuracy.

Whereas the Allied troops were, for the most part, wholly green, and led by inexperienced junior officers, the Germans, however odious the Nazi regime, were the best troops of their era. German troops were consistently surprised by the attitude of British soldiers, who appeared to them to be satisfied with doing the minimum required of them, seemed to be devoid of initiative, and were content to surrender as soon as their ammunition ran low. Early intelligence reports by the Germans noted the vulnerability of the English at close quarters. They also saw that the force used in attack was divided into assault groups under the control of officers. These officers were given their territorial objectives, and they would then relay these to the NCOs, without giving them any idea of the overall intent of the operation. Having taken local objectives, NCOs would dig in without exploiting the situation further. The Germans felt that if they could kill British officers, an attack would rapidly lose any initiative.

Fighting their way forward from village to village, the British advance on 6 June never gathered sufficient momentum to sweep on to Caen; the Canadian and British armour remained clogged-up in fighting around the beach-heads. The significance of Caen lay in the open country beyond it, ideal for tanks and airfields; it was a gateway to the heart of France and a thrust towards Germany. When the first day's assault failed to capture it, Montgomery launched three further attempts, in rapid succession. First, over 7 and 8 June, a direct assault was attempted. Despite valiant efforts from the Royal Ulster Rifles and the 3rd Canadian Division, the attack foundered at the western edges of the town. The Germans had been slow to mobilise their reserve forces, and no movements had taken place until several hours after the invasion. The Canadians then encountered the troops of the 12th SS Panzer, among whom were the fanatical teenagers of the Hitler Jugend Divisions.

The forces were of roughly equal strength, but the Nazis attacked the Canadians with stunning violence, superbly co-ordinating their armour, artillery and infantry. During the night of 7 June, a characteristic shock attack by SS Panthers penetrated right through the Canadian lines and enveloped a battalion headquarters.

Montgomery decided that a continued frontal assault on Caen would result in unacceptable casualties. He opted to tie down the Germans at Caen while making a pass to the west of the town, towards Villers-Bocage and

Battles

Evrecy, and then swing south-east, to Falaise and open country.

But to the German shield around Caen, composed of the 21st and 12th SS Panzer Divisions, had been added the considerable force of Panzer Lehr, which had raced overnight from Chartres. As the British 50th Division moved to the south-west of Caen, they were halted in the idyllic countryside at Tilly-sur-Seulles, and drawn into some of the bitterest fighting of the campaign. Here, amid the ruins of the village, Panzer Lehr endured night after night of nerve-shattering barrage and day after day of armoured assault. Montgomery then committed two of his veteran Eighth Army divisions, the 7th Armoured and 51st Highland, to the fray. The former would pass to the east of Caen to link up with a bridge-head made by the 6th Airborne; the latter would drive to the south-west. The town would be enveloped.

The attack to the east was conducted with great bravery, and great casualties, particularly among the lightly armoured British paratroopers. Though awful losses were inflicted on the Germans, the force of the attack was absorbed and it petered out. To the west, the forces made rapid progress on 10 June, but then foundered, as the infantry failed to take Tilly and numerous engagements with small detachments of Germans held them up. On 13 June the 7th Armoured managed to advance to Villers-Bocage, which they found unoccupied. They believed they had broken through the German lines. As the 7th Armoured took up positions, they suffered one of the most humiliating reversals of the entire war. A mere three Tigers, from the 501st SS Heavy Tank Battalion, ambushed the parked Shermans and Cromwells of the 4th County of London Yeomanry, blew up the tanks, machine-gunned the infantry, and utterly destroyed the British force. The British rushed reinforcements to the town, which was now under attack from two sides by units of Panzer Lehr. The British units clung to the town by their fingernails. The Germans, though outnumbered, succeeded in concentrating forces at crucial points to disrupt the British, who were thus prevented from uniting sufficient ground forces to penetrate. By 14 June, the British were disengaging from Villers, and had suffered bad reversals at the adjoining villages of Tracy-Bocage and Cristot.

The attempted envelopment was abandoned. Then, on 26 June, Montgomery launched Epsom, another attempt to encircle the German forces around Caen, this time between the villages of Carpiquet and Rouray to the west of the town. In the early morning, 600 tanks and 60,000 troops, supported by 700 naval and land guns, advanced across the countryside. For the most part, they moved in classic infantry formation, presenting a good target to the Germans. After three miles, the Germans again began to repulse them, and fierce fighting erupted all along the line. They clung on, and, after throwing back a German counter-attack the next day, tanks of the 11th Armoured Division finally broke through, only to be withdrawn when a British general decided that they were close to exhaustion. The attack had cost nearly 8,000 casualties.

Having united their beach-heads, the Americans fought their way towards Cherbourg, on the tip of the Contentin peninsula, through the thick hedges of the bocage. By 22 June the Americans were outside Cherbourg. Over the next ten days their troops, who had been trying to adjust to fighting in the maze of orchards and hedges, learned how to fight from street to street, and house to house, to take the immense concrete bunkers and fortifications the Germans had established. It took five days to subdue the Germans in Cherbourg, and more time to quell the resistance of isolated groups. Having taken the peninsula, the Americans began to press southwards.

THE BATTLE OF ARNHEM 1944. After breaking out from Normandy, Montgomery put forward an ambitious plan to outflank German defences by securing bridges across the Maas, Waal and Lower Rhine. In operation Market Garden, on 17 September, three airborne divisions – the US 101st and 82nd and the British 1st – were parachuted in between Nijmegen and Arnhem. The Americans took and held bridges over the Maas and Waal, but the British landed too far from the bridge at Arnhem to seize it with ease. They fought their way to Arnhem but were then attacked by the 9th SS Panzer, whom they repulsed in bitter fighting – so violent that the Germans were ultimately reluctant to engage them. As they held out against infinitely greater forces, an attempt by the Polish Parachute Brigade to relieve them failed, and on 25 September some 2,400 survivors withdrew by boat. The rest were firmly compelled to surrender. They lost 1,130 dead; 6,450 were taken prisoner. German casualties were over 3,000.

In early July, the British took the devastated town of Caen, but were still struggling to break through on either side of it. To the west, they fought brutal battles with the 12 SS Panzer (Operation Charnwood); despite outnumbering the Germans four to one in tanks and two to one in infantry, they made little progress. It was suggested that part of the British problem was the setting of limited objectives; battles were being fought for local gains. The invaders needed to by-pass the local defence and thrust into the heart of France. Montgomery now launched Operation

Goodwood. With the Germans tied up in fighting along the front, all three British armoured divisions – 8,000 tanks and armoured vehicles – would plunge through the Orne bridge-head to the east of Caen and, proceeding down a clear path cut by massive aerial bombardment, would drive for Falaise.

The attack was launched on 18 July. But the massive aerial bombardinent did not destroy the Germans; within hours, the three armoured divisions were stalled in fierce fighting. The light Allied tanks had advanced against well-defended sectors, without infantry support, and fell prey to anti-tank guns and hand-held weapons. Some tank units were losing half their vehicles. The operation was closed down on the night of 20 July, when heavy rain and mud made further progress impossible. The limited gains had cost 5,500 casualties and 400 tanks. In the aftermath, Montgomery, who had been publicly over-optimistic about the success of the operation, became the object of much criticism.

The American push south from the Contentin peninsula towards Avranches and Brittany was bogged down in the bocage. The Airborne Division distinguished itself in the fighting, but the rest of the infantry could not work up a sufficiently strong attack to make a telling breakthrough. In 12 days of fighting, the VIII Corps lost 10,000 men for a gain of seven miles. Some infantry divisions had effectively suffered 100% casualties. On 18 July the Americans drove back the German II Parachute Corps to take the heights of St Lo, which became the starting point for the most dramatic and successful of the American Normandy operations, Cobra.

On 25 July the US VII Corps attacked on a narrow 7,000-yard front, preceded by massive aerial bombardment of the German front lines, while the artillery shelled German positions to a depth of 2,500 yards. American armour passed cross-country to outflank the German positions. With most of their best forces tied up in fighting the British and Canadians, the Germans began to fall back. By 27 July the operation's first objective – the road junction near Le Mesnil-Herman – had been reached. The roads leading south-west became clogged with fleeing Germans, and burned-out vehicles. By the end of July the Americans were at Avranches. A reorganisation of their command structure resulted in the creation of Patton's Third Army, and, at the beginning of August, he pushed his tanks and motorised infantry over the bridge at Avranches into the Brittany countryside. It was a dramatic and impressive spectacle. Largely unopposed, they were outside the Brittany ports within days. The wisdom of committing such a large amount of forces to take empty countryside was nevertheless highly questionable.

On 6 August, in Normandy, the Germans launched Operation Luttich, a suicidal counter-attack near the town of Mortain by the exhausted elements of the XLVII Panzer Corps, which included the 1st and 2nd SS Panzer Corps and the 17th SS. They drove towards the coast, in an attempt to divide the American forces in Normandy from those in Brittany; Patton's spearheads were to be deprived of fuel and supplies. Hitler, increasingly insane after the attempt on his life, gave personal orders for the attack. But, possessing advance intelligence of the assault, Omar Bradley seized on it as an opportunity to destroy the German Army. The early German successes drove them into the open palm of the American forces; the palm closed into a fist, as the German armour was ravaged by Typhoons and Thunderbolts. The failed attack cost the Germans 100 tanks. But their deranged Führer, utterly divorced from reality, ordered another thrust towards Avranches. To find the forces for this, the Germans had to weaken the front at Caen.

The encirclement of the German forces was now well under way. Having penetrated south, the American XV Corps began to swing north again, aiming for Argentan, where it would unite with the British and Canadian forces, at last pushing south from Caen. But the Americans advanced more quickly than expected, and, with so many of their forces tied up in Brittany, were wary of their ability to close the trap and face the retreating Germans unsupported. They waited for the British and Canadians, and Bradley began to favour the idea of a "long envelopment", pinning the German forces against the Seine.

The British and Canadians had progressed south. There had been major changes in the command structure; after the débâcle of Goodwood, Montgomery had sacked a number of senior officers. Operation Totalize, a major thrust by Polish and Canadian armoured divisions towards Falaise, failed, and was immediately followed by another, Tractable, which took the Canadians to within a mile of Falaise on 15 August. But the attacks were hampered by the inexperience of the units, appalling weather conditions, difficult communications, erratic air support and, once again, fanatical defence from the SS units.

The Germans began, at last, to retreat out of the enclosing pocket. Their commander, von Kluge, was relieved of his position by Hitler and recalled to Germany. He committed suicide, as many of the defeated German generals would. But the Allies still failed to press home their advantage and close the pocket with due speed.

Hitler had authorised the retreat of the German Army. They were streaming eastwards through a gap which, by 19 August, was only a few thousand yards wide. But substantial German forces slipped through, while the Canadians and Poles were embroiled with the SS.

By 21 August the gap was closed. Tens of thousands of men and their vehicles emerged from hiding, threw caution to the winds and fled eastwards. Strafed from the air, shelled and bombed incessantly, burned-out vehicles and blackened corpses littered the fields and villages.

The SS Panzer crews reluctantly abandoned their burning tanks and began walking home to Germany. As the Allied forces moved into the pocket, they were awed by the spectacle; the roads were thick with the remains of grey-clad bodies and the corpses of horses and livestock caught in the withering bombardment. In the hot summer weather the corpses had become bloated with gasses, and exploded when the Allied tanks ran over them. They hosed the corpses with gunfire to release the gas before dragging them off to be burned. The air smelled so putrid that men wore gas masks as they advanced through the pocket. Thousands of dusty, shell-shocked Germans waited patiently to surrender, rather than escape and be compelled to fight another campaign as bloody as the battle they had just lost.

THE BATTLE OF THE BULGE 1944. On
16 December Hitler flung his last reserves of
250,000 men and 1,100 tanks into a
desperate attempt to strike through the
Ardennes and take the ports of Liège and
Antwerp, in order to split the Allied forces in
the north from those in France with the vain
hope of then "rolling-up" the front line.
Though checked by the US 5th Corps in the
north, the violence of the assault threw back
the US 1st Army and 8th Corps. But after the
Germans had reached Bastogne in the west
on 20 December, they were halted in the
south by the US 4th Infantry and 9th
Armoured. Patton's 3rd Army then attacked
the southern flank of the Germans' salient –
the "bulge" – and the German push to the
west was halted in front of the Meuse by the
British 29th Armoured and American 2nd
Armoured. Bastogne was then re-taken, and
Allied bombers smashed the German convoys
to cut off their supply lines. In January a
concerted counter-attack pushed the
Germans back, and, having failed to re-take
Bastogne, they retreated. By the end of
January they were back to their starting point,
at a cost of 70,000 casualties, 50,000
prisoners, 600 tanks and 1,600 aircraft. The
Allies lost 77,000 killed and wounded.

Chapter Nine

Berlin

We may be destroyed, but if we are, we shall drag a
world with us – a world in flames.

Adolf Hitler, 23 November 1939

On 16 January 1945, having overseen the abject
Ardennes offensive in the West, Hitler returned to the
German capital. He would never leave it again. Hitler's
decision to hunker down in his concrete bunker 55 feet
beneath the Chancellery ensured that the siege of Berlin
was the last great battle of the Second World War in
Europe. He had long prophesied a Wagnerian "last stand";
the battle of Berlin permitted him to turn his perverted
fantasy into the reality of Götterdämmerung.

When Hitler entered Berlin on 16 January, a gigantic
Russian offensive into east Germany was already four days
under way, involving the First Ukrainian front commanded
by Marshal Ivan S. Konev, and the First and Second White
Russian fronts commanded by Marshal Georgi K. Zhukov
and Marshal Konstantin Rokossovski respectively. Facing
these 2.5 million Russians, in Army Groups Centre and A,
were fewer than a million Germans. The Russian superiority in materiel was even more staggering: 6,500 tanks to
1,800, 4,700 aircraft to 800. Opening the offensive, Konev
disposed his artillery at 300 guns to each kilometre of front
– an artillery barrage that eclipsed anything of the hell of
the Somme or Passchendaele from World War I.

The Eastern Front collapsed like a house of cards. There
was fierce resistance from "Führer fortress" cities such as

Battles

Memel and Königsberg, but otherwise the only impediment to the Soviet advance was the attenuation of supplies. In a piece of typical military ineptitude, Hitler threw away 600 uncommitted tanks of the Sixth SS Panzer Army in a diversion near Lake Balaton in Hungary. The Red Army was not so easily deceived, and continued its relentless progress into Germany. Soon, Konev and Zhukov had reached the Oder and Neisse, and were posed to advance the last 40 miles to Berlin.

After pausing to re-supply (on a quite fantastic scale: Zhukov's front alone amassed 7 million shells), Konev and Zhukov's front crossed the Oder on 16 April for the final drive on the German capital. In the previous November, Stalin had promised Zhukov the honour of taking Berlin, but Konev's indispensable role in the advance to the Oder had caused the Soviet leader to rethink this wisdom. He decided to back both horses. After crossing the Oder, "Whoever breaks in first, let him take Berlin," announced Stalin.

The Russian commanders were under no illusions about the scale of the problem before them. The defense zone through which the troops would have to break extended all the way from the Oder river to Berlin – and Berlin on its own presented a formidable task. The Russian Army had never been faced with such a large and heavily fortified city. Berlin's total area was almost 350 miles square; there were great possibilities for underground troop movements in its subway and widespread engineering works; the city and its suburbs had carefully prepared themselves, so that every back alley and narrow canal was a part of its greater defensive plan.

Moreover, the German forces facing the Russian steamroller were not inconsequential, even if they only numbered 350,000 compared to Zhukov's 3 million. Berlin did not have its own garrison, and the only city-based unit of real value was the Berlin Guard Battalion (which had proved its martial worth as well as its political loyalty in its effective suppression of the July Plot). By default, the defence of Berlin fell to Colonel-General Heinrici's Army Group Vistula, which comprised the Ninth Army and Third Panzer Army, as the Russians pushed it into the city from its defensive line on the Oder. Of the forces at Heinrici's disposal, the most effective were the SS Nordland and 18th Panzergrenadier Divisions, together with remnants of the 9th Parachute, 20th Panzergrenadier, French SS and Walloon SS Divisions. The latter was led by Leon Degrelle, whom Hitler once declared his spiritual son. As for the rest of Army Group Vistula it was composed of a ragbag of units from the Hitler Youth, Volkssturm (home guard), military cadets, Luftwaffe ground personnel. Yet, some of these fought hard enough in the Seelow Heights on 16–17 April to bring Zhukov's advance to an ignominious halt. Envious of Konev's quicker progress towards Berlin from the south, Zhukov issued a terse set of orders to his commanders. The pace of the advance was to be stepped up immediately: a slow development would only serve to exhaust the troops and waste their ammunition. No commander was to remain in the rear of his troops, but should place himself at the observation posts of the corps commanders, and conduct the engagement in the direction of the main effort. All artillery was to be brought forward and remain no further than two to three kilometres behind the front line engaging the enemy. With this order, he reminded the troops that desperate resistance was to be expected, with the German Army fighting hard for every house – so tank crews and infantry were forbidden to wait for the "luxury" of letting the artillery wipe out the enemy before they moved forward. Finally, he ordered that no quarter was to be given, and the advance was to proceed by day and by night. For good measure, Zhukov also threatened that any commanders showing "lack of resolution" would be instantly dismissed. Zhukov's whip-cracking produced immediate results, and by the close of 19 April his army had blasted their way through every defensive line in front of Berlin. Konstantin Simonov, a Russian, encountered the remains of a German unit left in the wake of Zhukov's offensive:

In front of us lay Berlin, and to our right a forest clearing, now a chaos of jumbled tanks, cars, armoured cars, trucks, special vehicles and ambulances. They had uprooted hundreds of trees, probably in an attempt to turn round and escape. In this black, charred confusion of steel, timber, guns, cases and papers, a bloody mess of mutilated corpses lay strewn along the clearing as far as the eye could see . . . Then I noticed a host of wounded men lying on greatcoats and blankets or leaning against tree trunks; some of them bandaged and others covered in blood, with no one to tend to them.

On the following day, 20 April, the 6th Breakthrough Artillery Division began the bombardment of the Third Reich's capital. Colonel-General Chuikov of the Eighth Guards Army (the defenders of Stalingrad) was among those to watch the opening salvos:

A battery of heavy howitzers was stationed on an open grassy space beside a wood. Dark, ragged clouds were sailing across the sky. The earth seemed to doze, shivering a little from time to time from shellfire in the distance. The gun crews had already run out the howitzers, and were awaiting the command to fire. The muzzles were trained on Berlin . . . on the fortifications of Fascist Berlin – "Fire!" The heavy shells flew up, cleaving the air with a whistling sound. The path had been opened.

The city endured bombardment through the night, suffering heavy damags. In the morning, Chuikov returned to his observation post to view the devastation:

> Mist lay along the streets, mingled with dust raised by the previous night's artillery fire. In places the mist was overlaid by fat trails of black smoke, like mourning streamers. And somewhere in the centre of the city ragged yellow plumes rose skywards as the bombs exploded . . . Suddenly the earth shuddered and rocked under my feet. Thousands of guns announced the beginning of the storming operation.

The Soviet salvos provided an ironic salute for what was also the day of Hitler's 56th birthday. To mark the occasion, he granted Berliners an extra allocation of food and a special issue of stamps. In the afternoon the great and the bad of the Nazi regime gathered for a birthday reception in the surreal setting of the bomb-struck Chancellery. In the garden, Hitler inspected a line of troops drawn up for him, tweaking the cheeks of boy defenders of the Hitler Youth. It was Hitler's last public appearance. The Führer was not the human dynamo of old: observers remarked that he looked closer to 70 years old than 56. Decrepitude was threatening. Living on nerves and will, and medication of doubtful worth, the fires of his personality died down and flared up with worrying irregularity. The war was beginning to tell on him.

After inspecting the guard of honour in the Chancellery garden, Hitler and his entourage descended into the bunker for the daily situation meeting. Once again Hitler resisted pleas to leave Berlin. With the meeting over, the rats began deserting the doomed bunker. The first to go was Goering, his face glistening with nervous sweat, who told the Führer that he had "urgent tasks in south Germany". Reichsführer

Battles

SS Himmler left promptly on Goering's heels, also pleading urgent business (in fact, the continuation of his secret talks with the World Jewish Congress). Those of the hierarchy who remained behind in the fetid bunker were treated by Hitler's mistress, Eva Braun, to a birthday entertainment. Eva Braun swept up everyone she encountered and took them to the old living room of Hitler's apartment, which had managed to avoid bombardment and was still standing. Beautifully furnished in former times, it now boasted only a large round table, as everything else had been stored in the bunker – but the table was set out festively, and such luminaries as Reichsleiter Bormann and Theo Morell, Hitler's fat personal physician, had emerged from the bunker to celebrate. Someone had brought along a gramophone, but there was only one record to play – a catchy pre-war hit called "Red Roses Bring You Happiness". The guests danced and drank champagne and tried to laugh, despite the din of artillery outside that grew ever louder, rattling the windows.

By the morning of the 21st, Zhukov's tanks broke into the northern suburbs of the supposed Festung Berlin. Behind the armour, infantry units prepared themselves for urban warfare. The veterans of Stalingrad knew only too well how to go about the necessary business of besieging Berlin. Colonel-General Chuikov observed that an urban battle is governed by its own laws, being a fire combat that involves not only automatic weapons but powerful artillery and tank guns, all firing at targets only a few dozen metres away. Rather than a steady advance concentrated on one point, city battles are a jerky affair, as troops dash from one captured building to another, while defenders struggle to keep tactically important buildings from falling into enemy hands. The loss or gain of one such building is tantamount to the loss or gain of a stronghold – and such losses and gains take place on a broad front, on every street of the city.

Chuikov laid his plans accordingly. To force his way into Berlin, he formed assault groups, each made up from a company of infantry, supported by a troop of tanks or self-propelled guns, anti-tank guns, and platoons of flame-throwers and engineers. Over the heads of the assault group, artillery and rocket salvos prepared the stage for the next round of house-to-house fighting, while medical teams stood to the rear to deal with the heavy casualties street fighting engenders.

On the same day, the German high command (OKH) headquarters at Zossen, outside Berlin, fell to Konev's front. Zossen was abandoned without a fight; on the consoles of the teleprinters in the cathedral-like underground com-munications room, "Exchange 500", messages still spewed out from the unconquered parts of Germany. On the machines the absconding Germans had hung prim notices in schoolboy Russian telling the new owners: "Do not damage these installations."

In the Führerbunker under the Chancellery, Hitler was still in nominal control of the battle for Berlin. Still the micro-manager of old, he detailed with elaborate precision a final desperate blow to still the Red tide. An army group commanded by Obergruppenführer SS Felix Steiner was to sweep down from Eberswalde, north of Berlin, onto Zhukov's right flank. "The fate of the Reich capital depends on the success of your mission," Steiner was informed. Unfortunately for the Führer, Army Group Steiner was a figment of his imagination. It did not exist.

By the 22nd, however, some accurate perception of Berlin's real position finally permeated the bunker. The city was surrounded on three sides, and Zhukov's tanks were reported to be approaching the west side of Berlin. At the midday briefing, Hitler characteristically raged against the incompetence and cowardice of his military. Then, uncharac-teristically, he blurted out that the war was lost. Field Marshal

Battles

Wilhelm Keitel, head of OKW, and his chief of staff, Jodl, were given permission to leave the bunker and pursue operations as they saw fit. Hitler again declared that he would never leave Berlin: "Any man who wants may go! I stay here."

Despite the Führer's railings, the surviving German military formations near the city, General Theodor Busse's Ninth and General Walter Wenck's Twelfth Armies, were putting up a stiff effort to reach beleaguered Berlin from the west and south-east. Nonetheless, they were unable to prevent the Red Army from encircling the city on 25 April, at which Zhukov and Konev then turned their attention to the final stage of the battle: the advance to the city's centre. By Stavka Directive No. 11074 the thrust lines for the advance were delineated, with Konev's front aligned on the Anhalter station, leaving the capture of the pre-eminent symbols of the Third Reich, the Reichstag and the Chancellery, to Zhukov. Stalin had kept his promise.

Inside Berlin, the situation was desperate. The telegraph office was closed (after receiving a final message from Japan, wishing "Good Luck to You All"), water and public transport had broken down under the relentless bombardment, and food warehouses in the suburbs had been captured by the Russians. Most Berliners had gone underground into cellars, or flocked to the massive concrete flak towers which dominated the centre. Smoke from burning buildings hung over the city, whose rubble-strewn streets were eerily empty.

Among the few who did take to the streets were the flying court-martial squads of the SS Leibstandarte Guard Regiment, who shot or strung from lamp-posts suspected deserters. General Karl Weidling of LVI Corps was lucky to escape such rough justice. Charged with desertion by Hitler himself, Weidling rushed to the bunker to protest his innocence. Instead of a bullet, he was given a poisoned chalice – and made battle commandant of Berlin. Inspecting the city's defences on the 26th, Weidling found only cold comfort:

> The roads were riddled with shell craters and piles of
> brick rubble. Streets and squares lay deserted. Dodging
> Russian mortars we made our way to the underground
> station by jumps. The roomy underground station was
> crowded with terrified civilians. It was a shattering sight
> . . . Colonel Barenfanger, who commanded in this sector,
> pressed me for more men and more ammunition. I could
> promise him neither. Most of his men were Volkssturm
> troopers who had been sent into the exceptionally severe
> fighting with captured arms . . . No ammunition for these
> guns could be found in the whole of Berlin.

At the heart of Berlin's defensive system – such as it was
– was the Zitadelle, an island formed by the Landwehr
Canal in the south and the Spree in the north. Aside from
the remnants of Wehrmacht, Hitler Youth and Volkssturm
units tossed by the fortune of combat into the Zitadelle,
there was a substantial SS battle group under the command
of SS General Mohnke, consisting of 1,200 combat veterans
from the Leibstandarte Guard Regiment, Hitler's personal
bodyguard, Himmler's personal bodyguard, 2,000-strong
unit of Freikorps Adolf Hitler, together with fragments of
foreign SS divisions. Mohnke's battle group inflicted a
severe casualty rate on the besieging Red Army, perhaps as
many as seven to one.

It was never enough, of course. More than 460,000 Soviet
troops were blasting their way into the Zitadelle,
outflanking the street defences by smashing through
cellars, house walls and courtyards. There was little Berlin's
citizens could do but await their fate. Worn down by
months of continual air attacks, they now suddenly found
shells whistling over their heads. The defenders of the city
were Walloon Waffen SS, desperate men with nothing to

lose who fought to their last bullet, and fanatical Hitler Youth soldiers with 2-cm anti-aircraft guns – men and boys who were outgunned, running out of ammunition, under unstoppable fire. It was clear to all that whatever they could do, the end was coming.

Faced with their fate, there was nothing for the civilians to do but batten down and try to survive the final stages of the battle. This, though, was not a simple question of staying indoors and hoping for the best. Everything had run out. Water was in short supply; so was food. To get bread, a citizen had to join a queue of hundreds, sheltering under their steel helmets, outside a baker's shop in the small hours of the morning. This was no guarantee: supply could not meet demand, and often enough you would find yourself at the head of the queue with no bread left to buy. As the siege grew worse, bread became exchangeable for water – a half bucket for a loaf. These pathetic queues were no deterrent to the Russians, who continued their onslaught, but, driven by hunger, the civilians pressed against the walls as the shells exploded around them and remained in their places. Wooden Russian bi-planes sometimes cruised by at low altitude, machine-gunning the starving crowds. One civilian described the carnage:

> At the last moment the shopkeepers, who had been jealously hoarding their stocks, not knowing how much longer they would be allowed to, now began to sell them. Too late! For a small packet of coffee, half a pound of sausages, thousands laid down their lives. A salvo of heavy-calibre shells tore to pieces hundreds of women who were waiting in the market hall. Dead and wounded alike were flung on wheelbarrows and carted away; the surviving women continued to wait, patient, resigned, sullen, until they had finished their miserable shopping.

The situation worsened as the Russians pressed their advantage home. The air raids ceased as the front lines of Russians and Germans meshed together, indistinguishable from the air, but the artillery bombardment remained relentless, pouring into the city from three sides without a pause. T-52 tanks made their slow, inexorable way through the streets. The rattling of machine-guns and the whine of bullets was all around. There was nothing left to do but barricade yourself in a cellar and wait. Radio Berlin continued to broadcast until 24 April – though in the face of the nightmare, nobody seriously believed anything the Nazis could say. The final communication of Hitler's regime to its people was a tiny sheet of paper, the last newspaper of Goebbels's press, *Der Panzerbär* (the tank bear), announcing Goering's deposition and the removal of the "government" seat to Flensburg. The same citizen described the scene:

> The Russians drew nearer; they advanced through the underground railway tunnels, armed with flame-throwers . . . Exhausted German soliders would stumble in and beg for water – they were practically children; I remember one with a pale, quivering face who said, "We shall do it all right; we'll make our way to the north-west yet." But his eyes belied the words and he looked at me despairingly. What he wanted to say was, "Hide me, give me shelter. I've had enough of it." I should have liked to help him; but neither of us dared to speak. Each of us might have shot the other as a "defeatist".

On the 26th, Berlin's S-Bahn ring was breached. At the Anhalter station the Muncheberg Division, pushed back from its position at Tempelhof Airfield, came under attack. The Division's War Diary recorded heavy shelling, and other than that, a terrible silence, with sniping coming from many houses. A grinding artillery barrage came at dawn, driving them back through the streets, fighting all the way, until they arrived at the new command post in the subway tunnels under the Anhalter station. This railway station had become an armed camp. Under the crumbling cement ceilings, in the smoky tunnels, women and children huddled in corners listening to the terrible roar from above. Later that afternoon, the soldiers moved to change position, and were confronted with horror at the entrance: a heavy shell had broken through the room, squashing the terrified civilians against the walls below.

Desperate street-fighting around the shrinking central sector ensued, with the Russians rushing the Moltke bridge over the River Spree on the morning of the 29th, before assaulting the Ministry of the Interior building ("Himmler's House", as the Russians dubbed it). Once again the most committed of the German defenders were the SS splinters, now fighting amid the shell-struck ruins of their "Third Reich". Recalled one German soldier:

> The close combat boys went into action. Their leader was SS-Obersturmführer [First Lieutenant] Babick, battle commander of the Reichstag. Babick now waged the kind of war he had always dreamed of . . . He played the great general and treated everyone present in the dim candle-lit room to great pearls of military wisdom. He kept talking of final victory, cursed all cowards and traitors and left no one in any doubt that he would summarily shoot anyone who abandoned the Führer.

Babick's scheming took place not in the Reichstag itself, but in an air-raid shelter concealed in a cellar – even a fanatic could not deny that the city was under fire. Equipped only with an old sofa and a map of the centre of Berlin spread out over a dining table, Babick stayed at his post, never moving from the map, waiting for reinforcements – he expected new troops and even "Royal Tigers" [heavy tanks] to show up at any minute.

Babick was still bubbling over with confidence. For one thing, he thought himself perfectly safe in his shelter. SS sentries were posted outside, others barred the corridor to the Reichstag, and Royal Tigers, our finest weapons, were apparently just around the corner . . . Then an SS ensign, aged about nineteen, came to Babick with the report that Undermann and his men had come across some alcohol and that they had got roaring drunk . . . Babick roared out the order: "Have him shot on the spot!" Seconds later we heard a burst of fire from a sub-machine gun. The boy reappeared and reported: "Orders carried out." Babick put him in charge of Undermann's unit. Our ranks in the Reichstag got thinner and thinner.

During the night of the 28–29 the ebb of battle reached to a mere quarter of a mile from the Chancellery, underneath which Hitler was preparing the last day of his life. Another, more personal blow befell Hitler. "Der treue Heinrich" (Himmler) had been reported as seeking a surrender in the West. Goering had already been expelled from the Nazi Party and sacked as head of the Luftwaffe for having dared assume the succession to Hitler. To the drug-addled Goering, Hitler had been generous and spared his life. Himmler was accorded a different justice: he was expelled from the Party and his detention ordered.

At around one o'clock in the morning of the 29th Hitler married his mistress Eva Braun, in a bizarrely formal civil ceremony, performed by a minor official from the Propaganda Ministry, Walter Wegner, hurriedly summoned from his Volkssturm unit in the Zitadelle. Hitler and Braun both declared their pure Aryan descent and freedom from disease. After bureaucratically correcting the date on the marriage licence from the 28th to 29th, Wegner returned to his unit. An hour later he was shot dead by a Russian bullet. Meanwhile, in the bunker, the guests gathered for the Hitlers' wedding reception drank champagne and chatted stiltedly. Above them Russian shells brought sections of the Chancellery crashing to the ground, causing the bunker to shudder.

Leaving the melancholic reception party at 2 a.m., Hitler dictated his personal testament. Having learned nothing, Hitler's testament concluded: "Above all I charge the leaders of the nation and those under them to scrupulous observance of the laws of race and to merciless opposition to the universal prisoners of all people, international Jewry." Grand Admiral Dönitz was named as Hitler's successor as head of state.

Not having slept the previous night, Hitler withdrew to his private quarters. He awoke in the afternoon to more bad news – the execution by partisans of Mussolini and his mistress, whose cadavers had been hung by their heels from the roof of a Milan garage in a grim public exhibition. Hitler now earnestly set about his own suicide, testing a cyanide poison on his Alsatian bitch Blondi.

Late that evening Hitler attended the daily war situation conference, which was a mere formality, since the balloon which carried the bunker's radio transmitting aerial had been shot down and the telephone switchboard was inoperative. As to the battle inside the Zitadelle itself, General Weidling reported that ammunition and supplies were all but exhausted. Weidling bluntly told Hitler that within 24 hours the Russians would be at the Chancellery, and urged that the remaining troops be allowed to break out. Hitler dismissed the request. Eavesdropping on enemy radio stations confirmed to the defenders that Wenk's Twelfth Army was bogged down south of the Schielow Lake, while Busse's Ninth Army was now encircled. There would be no last-minute deliverance.

At 1.30 in the morning of the 30th, Hitler took his farewell from his female staff, silently shaking their hands. Then he took his leave of the male staff, in the same silent, shuffling manner, his vacant eyes thick with film. That the Führer was about to commit suicide was clear. After their initial incredulity the staff, a terrible presence of tyranny lifted from their lives, assembled in the canteen for a dance. Hitler himself slept fitfully for a few hours, before attending his last situation conference, at which the SS commandant of the Chancellery, Wilhelm Mohnke, reported that the battle of Berlin had reached Potsdamerplatz and the Tiergarten, only blocks from the Chancellery. Hitler received the reports without emotion, and then took lunch with his two favourite secretaries, Gerda Christian and Traudl Junge, and his vegetarian cook, Fraulein Manzialy. As they joylessly poked at their spaghetti and tossed salad, the fighting had reached the steps of the Reichstag, after a full frontal assault by three battalions of the Soviet 150th and 171st Rifles Divisions. Inside were positioned 5,000 SS, Hitler Youth and Volkssturm. High in the sky the sunlight failed to break through the cloud of black smoke that hung over the battle scene.

Two hundred yards away from the Reichstag, Eva Braun emerged from her quarters in the Führerbunker to join with Hitler in another farewell ceremony. Goebbels, Bormann, Krebs were among the senior members of the entourage still there; Frau Goebbels remained in her room, unnerved by her forthcoming poisoning of her children. Hitler and Eva Braun shook hands all round, and went back to their own suite. Most of the attendants were dismissed; only the highest-ranking and most necessary remained, waiting in the passage for the end of an era. A single shot was heard. The attendants waited a moment, then, at 3.30, entered the suite.

Adolf Hitler was lying on a blood-soaked sofa; he had

placed a gun in his mouth and fired. Eva Braun lay dead beside him. A revolver was by her side, but it had not been fired: she had taken poison instead.

The head of the Hitler Youth, Artur Axmann, was too late to witness the farewell ceremony. He arrived at the bunker a little later, and, in tribute to his status and contribution to the Reich, was admitted to the private suite to see the bodies. For some minutes he remained with them, talking to Goebbels. Goebbels then left, leaving Axmann to mourn with the bodies for a short while, while outside, another ceremony was being readied – a Viking funeral.

Finally two SS men, one of them Hitler's servant Linge, came to take the bodies. Hitler's mangled head was concealed as his body was wrapped in a blanket and carried out into the passage, his familiar black trousers making it easily recognisable even in its covered state. Two other SS officers carried the body four flights up to the emergency exit, and out into the garden, where petrol was waiting. Eva Braun's body followed – this time with no blanket, as her death had left a pristine corpse. She was passed from man to man: from Bormann, who took her from the room, to Hitler's chaffeur Erich Kempka, who carried her to the foot of the stairs, to Hitler's personal adjutant Otto Guensche, to a third SS officer who brought her upstairs.

The funeral pyres were meant to be witnessed by worthy eyes only. Unfortunately, a careful precaution – the locking of the other bunker door that led to the Chancellery and some of the doors leading there from the garden – led to an unauthorised intrusion. Erich Mansfield, a police guard, was on duty in the concrete observation tower at the corner of the bunker, and seeing through the smoke a sudden shutting of doors by furtive, hurrying men, he felt it his duty to investigate. Climbing down the tower into the garden and heading to the emergency exit, he collided with the emerging procession – with the unmistakable black trousers and unwrapped corpse of Eva Braun making it clear what was afoot. Mansfield was hastily banished back to his tower.

Having sent off the intruder, the ritual carried on. The two bodies were laid side by side and doused in petrol. A Russian bombardment forced the mourners to withdraw a few feet to shelter under a porch, where Guensche dipped a rag in petrol, lit it and threw it out to the corpses. A great flame immediately enveloped them. The witnesses gave the Hitler salute, standing to attention, and then withdrew to go their separate ways. Guensche later described the ceremony to others who had not managed to attend: he called it the most terrible experience of his life.

While the bodies of Hitler and Braun burned, the Red Army was still clearing the Reichstag with hand grenades and sub-machines, until a little after ten o'clock a final assault allowed Mikhail Yegorov and Meliton Kantaria of the 756th Regiment to hoist a Red Victory Banner on the dome of "the lair of the Fascist Beast".

Hitler dead, the Reichstag taken. There remained only surrender or escape for the remaining defenders of Berlin, hemmed into four isolated groups in the city. Goebbels, appointed Reich Chancellor at the same time Dönitz had been nominated head of state by Hitler, immediately sent an emissary to Colonel-General Chuikov. Ar four o'clock in the morning of 1 May, General Krebs, the former Nazi attaché in Moscow, arrived at Chuikov's command post near Tempelhof Airport. There a four-sided conversation began between Chuikov, Krebs, and by telephone to Zhukov and to Stalin in Moscow. After expressing his satisfaction at Hitler's death ("So that's the end of the bastard"), Stalin informed Chuikov that there were to be no negotiations with Krebs, only an unconditional surrender obtained from him. For several hours Krebs wheedled and inveigled for a conditional surrender and recognition for the new Nazi government of Goebbels, but was obliged to return to the bunker empty-handed. Any remaining delusion in the bunker that its inhabitants might be recognised as a sovereign government were ended at 6.30 p.m. on 1 May when Chuikov sent out the order to his troops: "Pour on the shells . . . no more talks. Storm the place."

Magda Goebbels took the thunderstorm of shells on the Chancellery area as her cue to poison her six children, before joining her husband in the Chancellery garden, where they took cyanide. Like Hitler, Goebbels made doubly sure of his demise by shooting himself in the head as he bit on the capsule. An ineffectual effort was made to burn their corpses, but the bunker inhabitants now had their feverish minds concentrated on their own destinies. Some, like Krebs, committed suicide. Most attempted escape. At 11 p.m. on 1 May, SS General Mohnke, the bunker commandant, led the first escape party out of the bunker complex, via the fire brigade station on Wilhelmstrasse. The scenes that confronted them seemed straight out of Dante's Inferno. By the light of flaming buildings Berliners were cutting up dead horses for meat, and drunken Russian soldiers chasing a naked woman across the rooftops, until she plunged five storeys to her death. Mohnke encountered a silent, moonless city, dark as pitch, lit only by the red light of the flares and shell bursts. A steady breeze blew through the yellow smoke; on the rippling surface of the river glimmered the reflected image of the burning buildings.

Mohnke's escape party only reached as far as the gigantic Schultheiss-Patzenhof brewery, where they were caught. After wining and dining Mohnke, the NKVD flew him to the Lubyanka prison in Moscow.

It was left to General Weidling, the commandant of the Berlin fortress, to organise the city's surrender. At 6 a.m. on

2 May Weidling and his senior staff passed through the Russian lines to Chuikov's HQ, where Weidling tearfully dictated the capitulation signal to his troops. Declaring that the Führer had taken his own life and left his loyal troops alone, he explained that Hitler's orders had been to fight on for Berlin, even without ammunition. This, Weidling concluded, was senseless. He gave the order: cease resistance forthwith. He signed the letter "General Weidling, General of Artillery, former Commandant of the Berlin Defence Zone". Chuikov changed just one word of the surrender order. He deleted "former" from Weidling's title.

At 3 p.m. on the afternoon of 2 May Soviet guns ceased to fire on Berlin. An enormous silence descended on the city.

It was the silence of the graveyard. About 125,000 Berliners had died in the siege, a significant number of them suicides, including Martin Bormann whose body was found during excavation works at the Lehrter station in 1972, fragments of a cyanide capsule still caught in the skeleton of his jaw. For Mother Russia, Operation Berlin had cost 304,887 men killed, wounded and missing.

Only the great encirclement battles of 1941 had cost her more.

Chapter Ten

Vietnam

On 30 April 1945, an American officer from the Office of Strategic Services (OSS), looking to establish a network of agents in Japanese-occupied Indochina, arranged a secret meeting on the Chinese border with a man who went under the name of the "General". The elderly guerrilla claimed to lead a network of fighters dedicated to the liberation of the Vietnamese nation. Since they had driven out the Chinese in 939 and established their own kingdom, the Vietnamese had for centuries suffered under invaders: the Chinese again, then the French and now the Japanese. This frail old man, whose real name was Nguyen That Thanh, but who had taken the title Ho Chi Minh ("He who enlightens"), had fled his country 35 years before and wandered the West, becoming respected as an intellectual who campaigned relentlessly for the emancipation of his race. To Western minds, he was a strangely contradictory man; a Communist, he believed passionately in the values embodied by America, and it was to that bastion of democracy that he looked for help. It struck those who encountered Ho Chi Minh in the early years that he was a Vietnamese Nationalist, and that his Communism was not the expansionist doctrine of a Stalin, but was the means by which a nation without a state expressed their collective suffering, and channelled their collective will to prevail.

It was 35 years later, to the day, at 7.35 a.m. that the last helicopters left the roof of the American Embassy in Saigon, taking the Americans out of a city besieged, and a war lost; a war which had cost the lives of 57,000 Americans, and 2 million Vietnamese. As the helicopters flew out towards the aircraft carriers waiting in the South China Sea, a Soviet-made North Vietnamese tank was ramming the embassy gates. For the Americans, the great disaster was finally over.

It need not have been the case. As the Americans had fought throughout 1944 and 1945 to clear the Japanese from the Pacific, President Roosevelt expressed the opinion that, were it not for the colonial ambitions of Holland, France and Britain, South-East Asia would not have been an unstable area, the Japanese would not have arisen as a power and Americans would not have been dying. Of Indo-China, he said: "France has had the country, 30 million inhabitants, for nearly one hundred years. And the people are worse-off than they were at the beginning."

He – and many others – believed that the Americans had a duty to bring relief to these nations, but had no wish to sacrifice American lives so that Holland, Britain and France could resume their colonial rule. Perhaps, he suggested, the nations could be under some international trusteeship until they had stabilised. He had no desire to impose a solution on Indo-China. But Roosevelt's pleas to his allies to allow the Vietnamese the right of self-determination went unheeded.

Roosevelt died, and Ho Chi Minh's provisional government of the newly liberated Vietnam immediately came into confrontation with the French, who made strenuous attempts to restore their authority by military force. They justified their violent intervention by expressing concern over the spread of Communism. De Gaulle told *Le Monde* the truth: "United with the overseas territories she opened to civilisation, France is a great power. Without these territories she would be in danger of no longer being one."

As time passed, the American involvement with France in the European theatre would lead to the acceptance that Vietnam was to be denied autonomy.

Initially, the country was divided, with the British Army occupying the South under the Potsdam Agreement, while Ho's forces held the North. Ho established a republic. Furthermore, he told the Americans that though hitherto nominally a Communist, such policies were to be subordinate to his republican nationalism. But, though the Americans could see no alternative to Ho as a leader of the nation when the French disappeared, the Great Powers did not recognise his republic. The British released French troops imprisoned by the Japanese, and the French assumed control of the South. In the North, Chinese Nationalist forces swept through the countryside. The country was in chaos.

In 1946, in order to get rid of the 200,000 Chinese troops in the North, Ho agreed terms with the French. Vietnam was to be a "free-state" within the French Union; 15,000 French troops would be stationed in the North, and the Viet Minh would cease fighting in the South. But eight years of bitter struggle would follow. The French lost nearly 80,000 troops in Vietnam, and never secured control of the country. Their battle only militarised the North Vietnamese and drove them into the arms of Russia.

It was at this time, with fear of Communism heightened by the Korean war, that the first American military aid began to flow to the French and their Southern Vietnamese administration; a modest $10 million in 1950. Ironically, Roosevelt's disparaging view of the situation was echoed by Senator John F. Kennedy, who visited Vietnam, and noted that America had "allied itself to the desperate effort of the French Regime to hang on to the remnants of an Empire". Kennedy would later take America further into the mire.

Battles

The French nemesis came in 1954, at the battle of Dien Bien Phu. After fifty-five days and a final attack lasting two days and nights, surrender to the Viet Minh came on the evening of 7 May. Two months later, at Geneva, Vietnam was officially divided into North and South, and the French began disengaging. Ho Chi Minh made a considerable concession in agreeing to the partition; it was known that if he had held out for immediate national elections the country would have been reunified. Still, the agreement allowed for joint North/South elections to be held in the future, with reunification possibly to follow.

Now preoccupied by the spread of Communism throughout Asia, the Americans began to replace the disappearing French in South Vietnam. The alliance between South Vietnam and America was initially centred on the figure of Ngo Dinh Diem, the contradictory and corrupt President – the man who coined the term "Vietcong", by which he meant all Vietnamese Communists, guerrillas or North Vietnamese. Before the border was established, Diem encouraged massive Catholic emigration from the North, and then told Hanoi, the North's capital, that there would be no joint elections; South Vietnam would establish its own Parliament. Through a rigged plebiscite, he established his presidency, and embarked on a tyrannical purge of opponents. The North still hoped that the international community would impose a political solution, and there was no immediate resumption of the guerrilla war. Diem built up an army of 135,000, which the Americans trained, but he wanted further American involvement in terms of money and materials. Initially withheld, this was forthcoming after guerrilla attacks on US installations in October 1957.

By the end of the decade, the North Vietnamese were infiltrating the South in large numbers, preparing for a conflict that they insisted they had tried to avoid. In 1960 –

even as the Sino-Soviet split gave the lie to the notion that there was a Communist conspiracy to be faced – the Americans doubled their number of military advisers in the country, and began to intimate that the possibility of an attack by the North might necessitate the deployment of American soldiers. Diem was not keen on this. But he was rapidly losing control of his country.

Kennedy took office in January 1961, and inherited the expanding problem of Vietnam. Amidst the conflicting advice, the most potent words were those of outgoing President Eisenhower, who expounded the "Domino theory", raising in Kennedy's mind apocalyptic visions of Communism breaking out in Australia and New Zealand. De Gaulle had been taught caution by bitter experience. He warned Kennedy that involvement in Vietnam would suck America inexorably into a "bottomless military and political quagmire". Privately, Kennedy had forebodings about committing further resources, and sending the troops, to Vietnam. But, while he contemplated withdrawal, he was suddenly confronted with the Bay of Pigs fiasco. The American disaster there made it impossible for him to accept a humiliating climbdown in Vietnam. Inevitably, a military solution was sought to an essentially political problem.

On 11 May 1961, President Kennedy ordered 400 Green Berets Special Forces and 100 military advisers to South Vietnam, raising the unofficial estimates of the American military presence to 2,000. These soldiers were to train the now 320,000-strong army of South Vietnam. Kennedy hoped that victory in any conflict would be possible without the direct involvement of American forces, but his chief military adviser, General Maxwell Taylor, argued that the Americans would have to provide up to 8,000 soldiers. The next May, the Americans dispatched a small force of naval and ground personnel to Laos, arguing that

Battles

Communist forces within the country and in North Vietnam were attempting to engineer the overthrow of the Laotian Government. Kennedy termed this mission "an act of diplomacy". By early 1962, the American presence in Vietnam had risen to at least 4,000, including 300 helicopter pilots. The Americans were officially only training, and leading the AVRN (the South Vietnamese Army) into battle, but officers and helicopter pilots were drawn into the shooting.

Much of the struggle against the growing guerrilla insurgency was based around the manipulation of the peasant population. The Americans now advocated programmes to teach the 17 million peasants how to defend themselves from guerrillas. They also created "strategic hamlets", designed to offer protection against guerrillas. But under Diem's regime, these processes were conducted in an autocratic and often savage manner. The Americans became desperate to see some effort from Diem to democratise the country; instead, his regime deteriorated into open oppression. In the summer of 1963, in protest at repressive measures taken against them, Buddhist monks began to immolate themselves in public. These images flashed before the eyes of the world. The Americans were thought to be supporting a tyrant.

In November 1963, Ngo Dinh Diem and his brother were assassinated in the course of a military coup headed by General Duong Van Minh. The CIA actively encouraged the overthrow, though it was not their intention that Diem should die. Now, as South Vietnam passed rapidly through the hands of successive governments, the Americans realised they had precipitated a crisis which would oblige them to become further involved. The North Vietnamese ran their forces down the Vietnam–Laos–Cambodia border – the Ho Chi Minh trail – in preparation for war. It was a point of no return for Kennedy; he agonised about withdrawal, and decided that Americans would begin coming home on 3 December. On 22 November 1963, he was assassinated in Dallas, and Lyndon Baines Johnson became President.

The Vietnam war killed Johnson. Its treacheries, deceits and reversals plagued him from the moment he took office, and utterly destroyed his presidency, his health, and his democratic dreams of a "Great Society". Although he was instinctively opposed to further involvement – particularly any use of combat troops – he found himself immediately pressurised by the "dynamics of military involvement" and obliged to conduct an aggressive course of action that would defend the reputation of the Democratic Party at home.

Within days, Johnson was committing the first of his great series of public hypocrisies. Although US support for the Saigon junta would continue, he announced, the first-stage withdrawal of American troops would take place; 1,000 would come home. Privately, Johnson agreed with the military that these should only be support staff, who could be quietly replaced at the first opportunity. Military preparations in Washington quickly extended to plans beyond the existing fighting.

In February 1964, AVRN generals publicly expressed the desire that the South should invade the North, with US support. Washington did not distance itself from such aggression, and guerrilla activity spread to Saigon, where American installations and bars were attacked. The US Defence Secretary, McNamara, spoke of the need to take "all necessary measures" to prevent a Communist victory, and the number of troops reached 23,000. Urged on by McNamara, who believed that air-power alone might win the conflict, the Americans evolved a two-phase bombing plan. Phase one was retaliatory, consisting of strikes against the North's military installations and guerrilla bases on the

Battles

Laos–Cambodia–Vietnam border, and was to be initiated in response to attacks on American installations or units. Phase two was a programme of intensive bombing in the North. A target list was drawn up, and it was calculated that, with saturation bombing and bombardment by the 6th Fleet, all North Vietnamese facilities servicing the guerrilla struggle in the South could be wiped out in 12 days.

Johnson accepted the plans, and authorised an increase in covert operations by the CIA against North Vietnam and Communist insurgents in Laos. Using the Canadians as an intermediary, the Americans communicated their intentions to the North Vietnamese, and intimated that if the battle to unite Vietnam was renounced, economic benefits would follow. The North Vietnamese Premier, Pham Van Dong, reiterated that the North sought a peaceful resolution, but that "the affairs of the South must be arranged by the people of the South"; the Americans must withdraw, and the military regime disappear.

In early August 1964 the North Vietnamese attacked American destroyers in the Gulf of Tonkin. In retaliation, President Lyndon Johnson authorised air strikes on North Vietnamese oil tanks and torpedo boats based at Vinh. The incident provided a spring-board for greater American involvement. On 7 August 1964, Congress overwhelmingly agreed to Johnson's demands for emergency powers to deal with the escalating situation in Vietnam. In response to Viet Cong attacks on installations, more frequent and heavier bombing was initiated; this was the second phase, operation "Rolling Thunder".

The bombing was not effective; the North Vietnamese and Vietcong guerrillas shifted installations, concealed weaponry and were undaunted by their casualties. Field Commander William Westmoreland said that America would have to enter the ground war. The American Ambassador, Maxwell Taylor, counselled against sending

South Vietnam, United States riflemen

in the troops: ". . . the white-faced soldier cannot be assimilated by the population; he cannot distinguish between friendly and unfriendly Vietnamese; the Marines are not trained or equipped for jungle warfare . . ."

On 8 March 1965, a flotilla of landing craft hit the beaches at Da Nang, and 3,500 Marines raced ashore to secure their beach-head and adjacent airfield. They were, Johnson told the public, only going to provide "base security"; they would not be used in offensive operations.

In a bizarre confrontation that encapsulated the hallucinogenic nature of the conflict they were being pitched into, they encountered no suicide squads of Viet Cong, but welcoming committees and swarms of beautiful girls who draped them with garlands of flowers as batteries of television cameras rolled. The American authorities wanted everyone to know that their boys had stormed the hostile shore in the defence of liberty. The TV war had arrived. Trained to immediately expect the terrors of war, the GIs were bewildered; Vietnam looked like a paradise.

Even before the first Marines hit the beaches, Johnson was pressing Congress for another 48 battalions. Within six weeks, the two "base security" battalions would swell to 80,000 ground troops, rising to 120,000 within four months, 300,000 a year later and a peak of 543,000 in 1969. Nearly 3 million GIs were "rotated" through 'Nam on 12-month stints of service. For most it was a blur, as they were rushed by helicopter from jungle to beach to military camp.

Only a quarter at any time were engaged in combat assignments, and only about 5% were actually fighting at any one time; many never saw much beyond their stockades. The rural Vietnamese – whose black pyjamas, mistaken for guerrilla clothing, had already made them targets for American hellicopter pilots – would remain utterly immobile when GIs arrived in their villages. Mute and untrusting, they froze, believing that any movement would result in their deaths. The gap between the cultures was never bridged; few GIs spoke any Vietnamese, and they were housed at a distance. When the two worlds did meet it was in a nexus of prostitution, drugs and material excess.

Around each American base grew a second city, built out of refuse and packing cases, where the Vietnamese lived, and where the American GI could buy, for a few dollars, anything the appetite desired; from a full valet service to sex and drugs. A vast black market quickly evolved in stolen American goods: cigarettes, alcohol, stereos, guns. The population of the cities swelled 600%, as the poor rushed to capitalise on the American gravy-train. Saigon and Cholon decked themselves out in cheesy Americana. By 1966, 30,000 prostitutes were plying their trade in Saigon. Outside the diplomats' villas or the bright night-clubs, the cities were dark and violent and disease-ridden. Outbreaks of typhoid, cholera and even bubonic plague swept the population; by 1966, one in four GIs had venereal disease.

The 500,000-strong AVRN proved increasingly ineffective in combat. Confronted by the affluence of the Americans, the morale of the underpaid AVRN forces collapsed still further. The Americans assumed more of the burden of combat.

General William Westmoreland isolated the problem area as the "politically pliant" Laos–Cambodia border, along which, via 1,000 kilometres of mountain trails, the North supplied the Viet Cong guerrillas in the South. Westmoreland believed that his enemy was already over-extended, and could be broken if denied the protection of rural areas around this border. Around 40% of the interior was uninhabitable jungle, swamp and scrubland, covered with elephant grass, a landscape in which the guerrillas had to be hunted down.

Battles

GIs went into combat, officially, on 27 June 1965, when forces launched a "Search and Destroy" operation north of Saigon. It was a month before Johnson told the American public, and intimated the vast numbers he intended to send to Vietnam.

August 1965 saw a rapid escalation of the ground war. At Chu Lai, an enclave on the coast, landing Marines had immediately found themselves engaged in a major fight with encroaching Viet Cong. The Marines had deployed troops by helicopter to drive the guerrillas against the shore, and then used the new forces pouring in from the sea – including amphibious tanks – to entrap the enemy in a system of caves. Shelled from the sea, and napalmed from the air, the Viet Cong melted away. The Marines lost 45 men, and reported an enemy "body count" of nearly 700. Westmoreland was hugely encouraged by this action, which he believed showed the mobility and concentrated firepower by which Americans could "attrite" the enemy and win the war. Helicopters would be the key to this. A week after Chu Lai, the 1st Cavalry Division, now totally re-modelled for rapid helicopter deployment, came ashore at Qui Nhon and moved inland to protect the town of Pleuhu in the Central Highlands. In the Ia Dran Valley, in the course of operation "Silver Bayonet", they fought a fierce battle with units of the infiltrating North Vietnamese Army. They claimed a body count of 1,771; but their own losses were 300, much higher than anticipated. The early optimism of Chu Lai was to fade quickly.

Westmoreland adopted a twofold plan. First, to halt the collapse of the AVRN and the Communist advance, which would take until the end of 1965. Then, having built up a sufficient logistical base, to launch an offensive, with the Americans conducting expanding "Search and Destroy" missions, driving the guerrillas into open battle, while the AVRN won the "peace offensive" in the villages. Victory would come, he hoped, by the end of 1967.

By November 1965, protest at the involvement in Vietnam was already growing in America; 35,000 marched on the White House, and two men – a Quaker and a Catholic – immolated themselves in public protest. Aware of the corrosive effect the American presence might have on the social fabric of a poor nation, Johnson began an initiative to "win the other war" – that against poverty. In 1966, 750 million dollars was poured into the infrastructure of Vietnam, in order to build an industrial base in the South; it was only one-fifteenth of the military expenditure. It all vanished, and the billion dollars a year thereafter went the same way. It went into the pockets of the increasingly corrupt urban classes.

The "search and destroy" mission was the keystone of American tactics. The helicopter made it possible to establish "firebases", a system of hilltop artillery fortifications positioned in remote areas and supplied by air; the ground would be cleared for the "firebase" by a "daisy-cutter", a 15,000lb bomb which would simply blow the top off the hill. From the firebases, forward infantry patrols, acting as bait and protected by the artillery, would sally into the scrub and jungle. When contact with the enemy was established, they would call in the helicopter "Search and Destroy" battalions. The firebases were intended to channel the guerrillas into areas in which air and artillery strikes could be brought to bear. In the early days of the war the 1st Infantry and the 25th Infantry formed a "defensive donut" around Saigon, the 4th Infantry and the 1st Cavalry operated in the Central Highlands, while the Marines were deployed at strongpoints and firebases throughout the countryside.

The Americans had experience of jungle warfare, having swept the Japanese from the Pacific. In the opinion of Vietnam veterans, however, the very nature of the

Battles

American army was unsuited to the war. Their tactics were inflexible; their sophistication bogged them down; they were overloaded with equipment and moved slowly on foot; their helicopters announced their arrival. The more Americans there were, and the more hardware, the more energy had to be devoted to logistics rather than fighting. The North Vietnamese, while acknowledging the courage and training of the GIs, thought that they adapted badly to their new environment, were weak in the face of simple deprivations, and pitied them their profusion of equipment.

Although 57,000 Americans died, there were no conventional set pieces to which their deaths might be ascribed, and no territorial losses or gains against which such appalling casualties might be measured. The nature of the fighting in Vietnam scarred a whole generation of Americans; drug addiction during and after combat experience was rife, and many veterans required psychiatric treatment or lapsed into torpor and crime.

Trained in open warfare, they faced a conflict in which they rarely saw their enemy. As their companions died around them, many Americans descended into rank paranoia. It was not that they lacked courage; but the absence of a visible enemy led to the conviction that they were fighting some malevolent supernatural force, and to a growing sense of futility and pessimism.

Months would pass for patrols with only a fleeting engagement. Then, without setting eyes on the guerrillas, crude booby traps, mines and grenades would cause carnage. To overcome the terrors of such a war required experience; the American practice of rotating forces through Vietnam on a 12-month basis meant that those with combat experience were immediately taken away from the theatre of operations.

Previous wars had not only been fought against perceivable opponents, but for clear-cut ideological reasons; liberty for America, a world free from Fascism, a Pacific free of the cruel Japanese. American troops possessed an altruistic self-image, but in Vietnam found themselves vilified. They could not understand what they were in Vietnam for; after a while, neither could their leaders.

One of the largest of Westmoreland's offensives, Operation Attleboro, took place in the closing months of 1966, north of Saigon, in the heavily wooded area bounding the Cambodian border, where it was known that the Viet Cong had created a vast complex of underground tunnels. In fact, the Americans had little idea of the sophistication of these underground complexes, which could stretch for 20 miles; some communities had rebuilt themselves underground, creating homes, schools, hospitals, recreational areas and munitions factories. After a pounding by artillery and aircraft, 22,000 GIs were airlifted in. They searched for bunkers and sealed the tunnels with grenades, then pumped in oxy-acetylene gas which was exploded with dynamite. The operation lasted 72 days. Though a body count of over 1,000 was claimed, this hardly justified the time and human cost. Body counts, brandished as evidence of progress, were subsequently exposed as wildly inaccurate; the decimated population of a village would be claimed as enemy dead if one gun was found in the vicinity.

The Americans targeted the Ho Chi Minh trail. In 1966 the North Vietnamese sent 90,000 troops along this route, marching them through the silent, defoliated forests, eluding the air strikes and the ground patrols. In some places the trail was perceptible as a wide road, winding and twisting through the hills and forests; in others, it was a network of hundreds of tangled paths, covering the whole of the border region. Two years of bombing had failed to cut it; it was heaving with men, artillery and munitions. In an effort to block the route, the Americans began constructing the so-called "McNamara line", a system of minefields and novel defences. Construction was halted by the North Vietnamese attacks in 1967.

In 1966, over 5,000 GIs were killed; in 1967, this rose to 16,000. By January 1968, the Americans were desperate to try and force the enemy out into the open. As the French had before them, they sought a battlefield, and ended up with a siege: Khe Sanh.

Khe Sanh lay in the north-west corner of South Vietnam, adjacent to the north-south border and the Ho Chi Minh trail. A perilous place, surrounded by misty hills, it was only useful in that it possessed an old French airstrip. But, because the area was thick with North Vietnamese, the Americans had been patrolling the area since 1966, hoping that it might provide the setting for a show-down; they had fought several stiff engagements. In 1967, Marines occupied it for use as a forward base for patrols. They established a base on a plateau, 1,500 feet above sea level, a half-mile long and a quarter of a mile wide. To the north-west of the plateau were two satellite hills from which the airstrip and plateau could be protected by a total of 46 artillery pieces. By early 1968, the electronic sensors dropped throughout the neighbouring countryside indicated that the Marines were being surrounded. The Viet Cong-occupied hills, between six and fourteen miles away, were bristling with artillery, and patrols emerging from the American base came under increased sniper fire. Between 15,000 and 20,000 elite North Vietnamese – including divisions who had fought at Dien Bien Phu – had slipped down the trail. The Americans put 3,500 Marines and 2,100 AVRN Rangers in the base, but they soon suspected that the countryside might contain up to 80,000 insurgents. Here, at last, for Westmoreland and the GIs was a chance to outface their elusive enemy and show what they could accomplish in open combat.

On 21 January 1968, the North Vietnamese began shelling

the base. On the first day, 18 Marines were killed, and another 40 injured; in addition, a direct hit on the main ammunition dump created a fireball as 1,500 tons of explosives blew up.

The Americans responded by firing 2,000 rounds a day at the North Vietnamese. But, as at Dien Bien Phu, their artillery was safely concealed inside caves. In February, the enemy began to launch ground assaults on the two satellite hills. They broke through the perimeter of Hill 861, closest to Khe Sanh, before being repulsed in two days of costly fighting.

At the end of January, the North Vietnamese launched the Tet Offensive. Up to 80,000 guerrillas and North Vietnamese regulars suddenly cast off their peasant disguises and attacked installations in every major Southern Vietnamese town and city. Within days, the GIs on the base at Lang Vei near Khe Sanh were horrified to see Soviet-made PT-76 tanks rolling towards them. The 1,000 defenders, Americans and Montagnard militia, fought valiantly, but only 24 GIs escaped.

The Tet Offensive cost some 2,500 American lives. For some hours, the North Vietnamese were inside the grounds of the American Embassy in Saigon, with the assembled TV cameras beaming home a savage gun battle in which no quarter was shown by either side. Finally, after fanatical street fighting between the Marines and 12,000 besieged North Vietnamese in Hue, the Tet Offensive was put down.

Halfway through the siege, America's weekly deaths in combat hit a new peak: 543 men. Within two days, another Marine patrol at Khe Sanh was ambushed with the loss of 23 men. The USAF lost its 800th aircraft. On paper, Westmoreland argued, it could be demonstrated that the Tet Offensive had cost the North Vietnamese 37,000 men, and shattered their strength. Westmoreland asked for yet more troops; instead, he got the sack.

Battles

The bodies poured back to America in canvas bags inside reusable aluminium containers. They were placed in burnished oak coffins, draped with the flag and delivered to the families at the rate of one every half-hour. Johnson could stomach no more of this slaughter. On 31 March, as the siege of Khe Sanh was lifted, he appeared on television, to announce that he intended to freeze troop levels, limit the air war and seek a negotiated peace; he also shocked everybody by saying that he did not intend to stand for President again. He would live another five, remorseful years.

At the same time – though the public would not know until the next year – Lt. W. L. Calley had led a platoon of troops into the village of My Lai. In four hours of crazed rape and slaughter, between 200 and 500 civilians – old men, women and babies – had perished.

With Robert Kennedy in the Democratic ascendancy, riding the crest of the national fatigue with the Vietnam war, it looked as if America might have an anti-war President by the autumn. But Kennedy was assassinated in Los Angeles, and the Republican, Richard Nixon, became President on 5 November 1969.

After a summer of fighting throughout the Central Highlands and Northern provinces, Johnson had announced that the Americans would no longer bomb North Vietnam. Now Nixon promised a phased withdrawal of American troops; 25,000 by June 1969, and another 35,000 by December 1969. At the same time an escalation of the conflict was planned, in an attempt to reduce the North Vietnamese position at the negotiating table. For the American troops, the disorienting stage of the war leading up to their disengagement was undoubtedly the worst.

The last batches of Marines to come to 'Nam brought the anti-war movement with them. Desertion rates rose dramatically; 245 illicit anti-war publications flourished. The final blow to morale came from an ill-advised decision by military commanders who, reasoning that the best thing to do was to keep the soldiers occupied, instigated a large-scale training operation, "Apache Snow". To their surprise, they ran into the North Vietnamese Army, firmly entrenched on Hill 937 – "Hamburger Hill". For ten days in early May 1969, wave after wave of the 101st Airborne Division were pressed into the assault, assisted by a million pounds of bombs and 150,000 pounds of napalm. The hill was taken at the 11th attempt, at a cost of 476 dead, and abandoned the next day. The enemy "body count" was 505. An illicit GI newspaper put a $10,000 bounty on the head of Lieutenant-Colonel Honeycutt, the officer who had ordered and led the pointless attack.

Bounties of between $500 and $1,000 for unpopular officers were becoming quite common. There were now too many inexperienced, ambitious officers arriving, eager to carve a career out of the wreckage of Vietnam. They demanded difficult objectives of their men, but often directed the assaults from the safety of helicopters. The GIs called the ever-expanding officer corps REMFS – "Rear Echelon Mother Fuckers". The result was open mutiny. In 1970, members of the traditionally fearless 1st Cavalry refused to fight on 35 occasions. It was not lack of courage, but a collapse of confidence in all they were fighting for. Furthermore, from 1969 onwards, "fragging" – the murder of unpopular officers – became commonplace. The term derived from the customary device employed, a frag-mentation bomb. Between 1969 and 1971, there were some 730 recorded incidents of fragging, and 83 officers were killed. But this does not include attempts on officers with guns, knives and hands, and only some 10% of suspected incidents of fragging were ever investigated.

As he took out the troops, Nixon widened the conflict,

Battles

taking it into Cambodia and Laos, and authorised two campaigns of strategic bombing, the secret bombing of Cambodia and the 1972 "Christmas" bombing of Hanoi and Haiphong. But, despite these initiatives and good resistance from the AVRN, the North Vietnamese continued to make ground, and now came out of cover to sweep over the border in large-scale conventional attacks, led by Soviet-made tanks and aircraft.

On 29 March 1973, following a ceasefire agreement negotiated between Henry Kissinger and Le Doc Tho, the American withdrawal was completed, without the US having obtained guarantees as to the security of South Vietnam; at the time, there were 150,000 North Vietnamese troops in South Vietnam.

The American prisoners of war held in Hanoi were released and the last GIs began their 9,000-mile journey home. A little over two years later, the helicopters would rise from the roofs of the US Embassy in Saigon, as the North Vietnamese drove through the remnants of the AVRN and toppled President Thieu from power.

Chapter Eleven

The Gulf War:
The Mother of
All Battles

Saddam Hussein's invasion and annexation of Kuwait in August 1990, provoked the largest concerted military action since the Second World War. As the Iraqis dug in along the Kuwait–Saudi Arabian border, and Hussein indulged in flagrant sabre-rattling, the Americans, acting under the aegis of the United Nations, brought together an extraordinary coalition of forces from the Christian and Muslim, capitalist and Marxist worlds. The first phase was "Operation Desert Shield", the securing of the Saudi border from further Iraqi encroachment. This was followed by the offensive stage, "Operation Desert Storm", the 100-hour war that swept the 500,000-strong Iraqi forces from Kuwait. The epithet "the mother of all battles" derives from the vague and rash threats made by Saddam Hussein as to the slaughter any attack would precipitate. In the event, Allied casualties in the ground fighting would be under 200, of whom a quarter were killed by their own side. The Iraqi casualties remain unknown to this day. Originally thought to be anything up to 150,000, they were more reasonably estimated at around 8–10,000.

The Americans provided the overwhelming bulk of men and munitions; over 400,000 troops. It was therefore an American, General Norman Schwarzkopf, who assumed the position of Supreme Commander. "Stormin' Norman",

Battles

as he became known, was a 56-year-old Vietnam veteran of considerable physical presence who possessed a mercurial temper; in a war which was fought under the constant gaze of television cameras, his ease with the media and gift for an apposite phrase was of enormous value.

The British, who sent the second largest contingent, about 40,000 troops (including the "Desert Rats"), were commanded by Lieutenant-General Sir Peter de la Billiere. De la Billiere had previously fought in the Middle East, spoke a little Arabic and knew from experience how to secure good relations with the Arab allies and hosts. Moreover, he had for many years been associated with the Special Air Service, the SAS, whom he had fought with in Oman and Malaya and commanded in the Falklands conflict. He had also planned and commanded the spectacular SAS seizure of the Iranian Embassy in London, after its occupation by terrorists. De la Billiere's appointment in another situation where hostages were involved – Saddam's "guests" being held as human shields at important installations – led to speculation that the SAS might become involved in rescue attempts. De la Billiere considered the possibility, but as the hostages were constantly moved, and intelligence inside Iraq was not good, such tactics were eschewed. Instead, the SAS – and American "elite" forces – were put to excellent use in covert missions in the Iraqi interior, where they hunted down Scud missile launchers. The Scuds were of vital importance; they were the means by which Saddam attempted to provoke Israel into entering the conflict, an eventuality that would have shattered the coalition. The American and British special forces also infiltrated Iraq to plant the homing devices which would guide the bombing raids preceding the ground invasion.

Another force in the conflict, and something of an ambivalent one, was the media. America had already fought a television war in Vietnam. Many American officers considered that the cameras had contributed to the loss of public and military morale, and hastened defeat. They were therefore uneasy about the presence of thousands of press. For the same reasons, the Iraqis welcomed the press into Baghdad before the hostilities; even after war erupted, they kept a crew from CNN in the city, showing them selected highlights of the Allied bombing campaign. Predictably, the media turned out to be a double-edged sword: quick to gloat over the boasted efficacy of Allied technology, and as quick to focus on its failures and the inevitable civilian victims of the conflict. But the vilification of Saddam was such that no unfortunate tragedy could undermine the campaign against him.

The deadline for implementation of the United Nations resolution calling for the withdrawal of Iraqi forces from Kuwait (Resolution 660) expired at midnight on 17 January 1991. Up until the last moment, the Russians, who were officially neutral, but in sympathy with the coalition, attempted to secure a negotiated settlement.

On paper, elements of the Iraqi Army, hardened by eight years of war against Iran, posed a considerable threat, notably the Republican Guards armoured divisions. To secure absolute victory in a campaign, it is thought that one should possess a numerical advantage of three to one. It was therefore with a grim realism that the Allied commanders feared that casualties might be as high as 40,000 if the campaign lasted for any length of time. However, against the numerically superior Iraqis, the Allies possessed better-trained, well-motivated professional forces – and a dazzling array of military technology. Iraq's forces were principally equipped with Soviet-manufactured arms, less modern and less efficient. The Soviet Union was happy to supply the Allies with details.

The first phase of the Mother of All Battles was a massive air campaign, designed to destroy Iraq's air defences, then key military, industrial and communication installations, and finally to deplete the Iraqi military forces by up to 50% to minimise Allied casualties.

In the first 24 hours of the air campaign, over a hundred Tomahawk Cruise missiles were launched from the American ships in the Gulf, and Allied aircraft launched the first of 110,000 sorties against targets throughout Iraq and Kuwait. British Tornadoes, equipped with the JP233, runway-catering bomb, conducted hazardous low-level runs against airfields. American "Stealth" bombers, invisible to radar, executed precision, radar-guided attacks with "smart bombs", reputedly so accurate that they occasionally put bombs down ventilation shafts or two within the same crater. Extraordinary though these feats of accuracy were, their frequency was afterwards much contested. Undeniable, however, was the courage of the Allied pilots, among whom the Tornado crews were particularly distinguished. They suffered the heaviest losses, as the low-level sorties claimed five aircraft within the first week. The efficiency of the JP233, designed to crater Eastern European tarmac runways built on solid ground, was called into question; much of its force was wasted on the Iraqi strips, constructed from a thin layer of tarmac spread over sand. The Tornado pilots would later successfully switch to medium-level bombing raids, employing laser guidance from specially imported, veteran Buccaneer aircraft. But, by then, their mission had been wholly accomplished; the Iraqi Air Force was neutralised within hours of the war commencing. The Allies were to lose a total of 67 aircraft. Some allied aircrew were captured by the Iraqis, and paraded on television, before being distributed around the country to discourage Allied attacks. It later transpired that most of these had been tortured. Other aircrews were successfully rescued by daring forays into the Iraqi interior.

On the second night of the air campaign, Saddam began

The Gulf War: The Mother of All Battles

firing Scud missiles, descendants of the Second World War V2s. Some of these were fired against Saudi Arabia, some against Israel. There was a very real fear that they might possess chemical or nuclear warheads. Though this was unfounded, Israel issued gas masks, and in the Saudi capital and Allied command centre in Riyadh, men were quickly sick of struggling in and out of their protective clothing. Fears that Saddam Hussein would use chemical and biological weapons against ground troops led to mass-vaccination programmes against such potential weapons as anthrax.

The six missiles that hit Israel in the initial attack killed nobody, and though Israel declared itself to be in a state of war, frantic diplomacy by the Allies managed to dissuade Israel from taking the immediate punitive action central to its foreign policy. Batteries of Patriot ground-to-air missiles

---

BATTLE OF THE 38TH PARALLEL. At the climax of the Korean war, 485,000 North Korean and Chinese troops attacked General MacArthur's 365,000 UN forces on 1 January 1951, capturing Seoul and Inchon. But Americans under General Ridgeway held, then counter-attacked, re-taking Inchon on 10 January. Ridgeway replaced MacArthur (who had wanted to widen the conflict to China), and checked a further Communist offensive, before the US 8th Army counter-attacked to drive the Communists back north of the 38th Parallel. By mid-July, the Communists had suffered 200,000 casualties, and were forced to come to the negotiating table. After lengthy talks, an armistice was finally signed in July 1953.

were dispatched to Israel. The Patriots were initially prone to malfunction, and several times released ineffective salvos. When they struck the incoming Scuds, they did not necessarily destroy the warhead. Air action – and covert forces operations – to reduce the Scud threat against Israel became an absolute priority. In the end, the Israelis suffered only two direct and 11 indirect fatalities from Scuds. The most effective Scud launch, from the Iraqi point of view, was that which, right at the end of the conflict, landed on a barracks in Dhahran, killing 28 American soldiers.

As the air campaign proceeded, Allied naval forces in the Gulf recaptured some offshore islands, and the Royal Navy Lynx helicopters, armed with Sea-Skewer missiles, effectively destroyed the diminutive Iraqi Navy; the Iraqis lost 143 out of 165 vessels, damaged or destroyed. The Americans, for reasons which would become apparent when the ground campaign began, gave much publicity to the arrival offshore of 17,000 Marines, who began practising amphibious landings. It was part of a deception plan in which the Iraqis were led to believe that the main Allied thrust would come from land and sea assaults on Kuwait City.

Retaliating in a customary, dirty fashion, Saddam ordered the release of vast amounts of oil into the Gulf. This, and the burning of Kuwaiti oil wells, he blamed on Allied air strikes. While some wells might have been ignited in the course of the conflict, the majority resulted from typical spite on the dictator's part. Some of the wells were to burn until November, turning the sky over the Middle East black with soot. The environmental damage was appalling.

On 29 January, the Iraqis mounted their only ground offensive of the war. Ten miles south of the Kuwaiti border was the abandoned Saudi town of Khafji which Saddam targeted as a propaganda exercise. An Iraqi force of tanks

The Gulf War: The Mother of All Battles

Saddam Hussein

and infantry sidled down the coast, the barrels of their
tanks reversed, as if indicating surrender; many of the
accompanying soldiers had their hands raised. Meanwhile
17 boats of Iraqi "commandos" attempted an assault by sea.
Although half the Iraqi troops were so ill-coordinated that
they never made the battle, and 14 of the attacking boats
were sunk, 400 Iraqi soldiers did manage to occupy the
empty town. The small Allied forward outposts had simply
withdrawn to await such a counter-attack. When it was
made, units of American and Qatari troops duly blasted the
Iraqis into surrendering the worthless town. The Iraqis lost
65 dead; the Americans 11 Marines, seven of whom were
killed in one "blue-on-blue" or friendly-fire incident.
Saddam hailed it as a crushing victory, and rained medals
on his coterie of sycophants.

Despite pressure to maintain the air offensive as a
means to force surrender, all the Allied commanders were
well aware that no war had been won through air action
alone, and plans for the ground offensive were well under
way. The strategy was built around an enormous deception operation. The Marines' landing exercises, and other
such activities in the Persian Gulf, were part of this. The
second strand was to convince the Iraqis that the bulk of
the Allied forces were simply lined up along the heavily
defended Saudi–Kuwait border, in preparation for a
frontal assault. To keep the Iraqi forces tied down in this
sector, an enormous electronic deception programme was
initiated, which created an illusory army. In fact, although
the 1st and 2nd Marines, the Tiger Brigade of the 2nd
Armoured and the Coalition Arab forces would assault in
this sector, Schwarzkopf had secretly shifted the bulk of
his forces over to the western flank of the battlefront, to
the Iraq–Saudi border. He intended to launch a three-
pronged "left hook", which would drive into Iraq, then
swing east to encircle the Iraqi forces in Kuwait and

destroy the Republican Guard divisions encamped around Kuwait City.

The western-most prong of the attack was to be made up of lightly armoured, highly mobile French forces, who would drive up to the Euphrates river to shield the flank of the second prong, the US XVIII Corps. This was made up of the 3rd Armoured Cavalry, the 101st Airborne and the 24th Mechanised. Equipped with Cobra helicopters, it would drive north of Kuwait City to cut off the Iraqis at the Euphrates and Tigris valleys. The third prong, the US VIIth Corps, among which were the British 1st Armoured, was the great steel punch of the attack. It included the 1st Armoured Cavalry, the 1st Armoured, 3rd Armoured and 1st Infantry – the bulk of the Allies' armour. This was to advance on Kuwait City, destroying the Republican Army divisions. The specific British task was to protect the right flank of the assault and destroy the Iraqis' tactical reserves. There was a certain amount of controversy over the inclusion of the British in this "left hook". Originally Schwarzkopf had placed them alongside the Marines, on the Kuwaiti front of attack. But de la Billiere, after considering the matter, had argued for a more prominent role for the British, which he thought politically vital. In addition, de la Billiere said that, since the British forces included their own infantry, they should operate independently of the Marines and fight the swift-moving battle they were equipped for. Privately he was also concerned to minimise casualties, and did not want to place his prize soldiers alongside Marines who, though fearless, had a reputation for injudicious actions. Though none too happy at the time, Schwarzkopf was fulsome in his praise for the British, describing their performance as "absolutely superb".

General Colin Powell, Chairman of the Joint Chiefs of Staff, later expressed his concern that the most dangerous part of the battle would not be the "left hook", where the speed and hitting power of the armoured and mobile divisions would be irresistible, but the secondary, frontal assault of the Marines and Arab forces towards Kuwait City. Absolutely necessary to tie down Iraqi forces, the attack faced much vaunted defences. The ground forces were concerned that the air force should have endeavoured to take out every piece of Iraqi artillery before the assault. The army used infiltration teams to assess these frontal defences, attack Iraqi strongpoints and attract the attention of artillery; when it opened up they would pinpoint it and bury it under rounds from the terrifying Multiple Launch Rocket Systems.

In the hours leading up to "G-Day", Marine bulldozers began to breach the Iraqi defences, knocking over the sandberms and filling in ditches. The trenches of oil were smothered or burned dry with napalm. As the hour of attack neared, a ferocious bombardment began, employing everything from B-52s to naval guns, and at 4 a.m. on Monday, 24 February, the Marines began to push through the Iraqi front line. The breaching operations were wholly successful, and in many places the Marines advanced well ahead of timetable. Enemy resistance was half-hearted, and their artillery fire sporadic and inaccurate. The minefields posed fewer problems than expected, since the sands had shifted, either exposing the mines or burying them so deep as to be ineffective. By night on the first day of the ground war, the 1st Marines had advanced halfway to Kuwait City. The next day, while the 2nd Marines pushed to positions west of Kuwait City, the 1st Marines fought a fierce battle with Iraqi units in the Burgan oilfield, close to the international airport. They flushed them out with a massive artillery barrage and then ravaged them with tank, helicopter and artillery fire; by early Wednesday the airport had fallen, and 100 Iraqi tanks had been destroyed.

The Gulf War: The Mother of All Battles

Their Arab Allies proceeded more circumspectly. For political reasons, the Syrian forces did not cross the front line until the conflict was two days old. The Egyptian forces were concerned about an Iraqi counter-attack, and established blocking points. The Saudis, in the east, prevailed against the Iraqi 5th Mechanised, but were delayed by the thousands of Iraqi soldiers who queued up to surrender. The Marines had no choice but to press on, though this meant that the coalition was closing on Kuwait City before the forces were in place to entirely envelop the Iraqi forces.

In the west, the "left hook" kicked off with a lightning assault by the French 6th Light Armoured Division. By the evening, they were in position to attack Al-Salman, where the 45th Iraqi infantry, who posed a threat to the Allies' left flank, were situated. The Iraqi division was caught on the hop, its guns pointing east at Kuwait, not south. The French and American 82nd Airborne pounded it with artillery and helicopter fire, then poured in tanks and infantry. By mid-afternoon the following day, the battle was over, with the Iraqis surrendering in droves. The French then set up a blocking position to defend the other two prongs of the "left hook".

The XVIII Corps began by establishing a base for airborne operations inside Iraq, and in the afternoon of the first day launched itself towards the Euphrates river. The speed of their advance was remarkable. A lack of enemy resistance advanced the timetable, and after a fierce fight between the 24th Mechanised and an Iraqi commando division at Talil, they had by the third day created a blocking point south of the Euphrates, cutting off Iraqi escape.

The great steel punch of the VIIth Corps began to swing into action a day earlier than planned, spurred on by deteriorating weather and reports of atrocities in Kuwait City. The 1st Infantry breached the diminished Iraqi defences, and the 1st British Armour rolled through, to be followed by the rest of the VIIth Corps. The steel fist, 60 miles wide and 120 miles long, careered into Iraq, devastating Iraqi forces foolish enough to resist. That day, the British suffered their worst casualties, when an American A-10 "Tankbuster" mistakenly wiped out a British Warrior Armoured Vehicle; nine soldiers died, in an incident which left a sour taste after the war.

Using the triumphant British forces as a pivot, the VIIth Corps wheeled east into Kuwait, where it made for six divisions of the Republican Guards. The Iraqis had assumed that the VII Corps would make for Kuwait City, and placed the Iraqi 12th Armoured to block the advance, intending to bring these six divisions down on the Allies from the north. Too late, they realised that the VII Corps' target was, in fact, the Guards themselves. Three guards divisions set up a blocking line, but, on the afternoon of 26 February, the divisions were utterly devastated by the VIIth Corps. Artillery, Apache helicopters and rockets paved the way for a final tank assault. The next morning, the remnants of the Guards divisions and the Iraqi 14th Mechanised attempted to fight a rearguard action, but were overrun in a fierce attack fought in a sandstorm.

By 26 February, 30,000 prisoners had been taken and at least 26 of the available 40 Iraqi divisions rendered ineffective or destroyed. The rest of the Iraqi Army was already in open flight; they had been pulling out along the Basra–Baghdad road since 25 February. The Allies pushed on, attempting to reach the road, cut off the Iraqi retreat and encircle the remainder of the Republican Guard, then deployed just within the Iraqi border.

Within 48 hours the Iraqi Army had disintegrated. They surrendered en masse, waving anything white they possessed. More than 370 Iraqi tanks had been destroyed. Saddam was desperately trying to retrieve what little was left of his army. By the night of 27 February he had lost 34 of his 40 divisions, and the Allies had taken 86,000 prisoners.

Outside Kuwait City, the 1st and 2nd Marines were poised for a final thrust. Their Arab partners were now making good progress, and Egyptian and Saudi forces were in the outskirts of the city. They had anticipated fighting a fierce hand-to-hand battle, but resistance was minimal. The previous day, Iraq's ambassador had informed the UN that Iraq had now complied with all UN resolutions; the last Iraqi had left Kuwait.

This was not strictly true; they were still in open flight. The Iraqis had begun to run up the Basra road so quickly that the Allied ground forces had not yet cut it off, but the air force had spotted a mass of vehicles speeding north. At first, it was thought that this convoy was trying to escape and link up with the Republican Guards; later it was realised that this was the remainder of the Iraqi Army attempting to escape, senior officers and all, with its arms intact, and absolutely glutted with booty. From 2 a.m. on 26 February, a dozen F-15Es bombed the front of the 1,000-vehicle convoy, near the Mutlas Pass, a chokepoint. They then bombed the rear. Whatever its intentions, the convoy was now trapped. Many sensibly fled across the desert; those who remained were attacked the following day by waves of American aircraft. The liberal hand-wringing that went on was in complete contradiction to the same liberals' desire to see Saddam's forces rendered impotent in the short and long term.

With the VII Corps still attacking the surviving Republican Guards divisions on the border, Schwarzkopf would have liked to continue the war for another day or two; the Allies' principal targets were not infantry, but tanks and artillery, and there were still tanks to be destroyed. But the coalition had to balance this need against the adverse publicity created by the media's pictures of the

Battles

Basra road; furthermore, Kuwait had been liberated, and the UN mandate only extended to this. It was decided to call a ceasefire at 8 a.m. on 28 February. "The Mother of All Battles" was over.

Chapter Twelve

Tora Bora

It started in 1989, but few noticed. An obscure Saudi-born religious fanatic called Osama bin Laden formed a terrorist group called al-Qaeda ("The Base"), which promptly declared a holy war or jihad on the West. Four years later, bin Laden financed his first attack on the World Trade Center in New York, which he followed up with bombings of US embassies and military facilities, including the USS *Cole*. These were but pinpricks upon an elephant's hide. Only when al-Qaeda turned airliners into bombers in its 11 September 2001 attack on the World Trade Center and the Pentagon did America and the West awake to the war against them.

Their retribution was swift. On 7 October 2001 President Bush launched "Operation Enduring Freedom", a massive offensive against al-Qaeda bases in Afghanistan. Since the Taliban rulers of Afghanistan were supportive of al-Qaeda they too found themselves in the sights of the Allied military. In the initial phase of Enduring Freedom, al-Qaeda and Taliban targets were subjected to a devastating aerial bombing campaign. The bulk of the ordnance used was 500-pound Mark 82 bombs, although Taliban and al-Qaeda front-line positions were also treated to the terrifying 15,000-pound BLU-82 bomb, known as the daisy cutter. Bombed by an enemy they could not see or fight, the Taliban, with their gold sandals and penchant for women's cosmetics, were soon in disarray. By early November, even the most limited Allied special forces operations on the ground, together with attacks by anti-Taliban Afghan

179

fighters, were enough for city after city to surrender. On 13 November the Taliban fled the Afghan capital, Kabul, to ecstatic celebrations by its citizens.

But al-Qaeda was made of sterner stuff, and fanatically resisted all attacks by Allied units. In the last days of November al-Qaeda massed at Tora Bora in the White Mountains, near the Pakistan border. Human intelligence (HUMINT) from captured Taliban, local villagers and Afghan militias indicated that bin Laden himself was at the Tora Bora cave complex, which had originally been dug and developed by the mujahedin in their war against the Soviets. Now it sheltered, alongside bin Laden, perhaps three thousand of al-Qaeda's best Arab, Chechen and Iranian fighters.

Tora Bora was never going to be an easy battle for the Allied forces. Much of the battlefield was near vertical, and thick with pine trees and snow. Moreover, local Afghan villagers, and even some of the Afghan forces ostensibly on the Allied side, were treating with al-Qaeda. Before fleeing to Tora Bora, al-Qaeda had helped themselves to a large portion of the reserves of the Afghan banking system. Not a few al-Qaeda, deciding that discretion was better than a martyr's trip to heaven, bought taxi rides to Pakistan at up to $500 dollars a head. Bin Laden, unknown to the Allies, was among the first to leave. Indecision and overcaution by the Allied military command, headed by US General Franks, failed to plug the exit routes out of Tora Bora, particularly to the south.

Tora Bora should have been a death trap. In the event it was a sieve.

Not that dramatic fighting was to be in short supply. On 30 November the US Air Force began the heavy bombing of the cave complex, while US Special Forces were inserted into the battle zone by helicopter to oversee raids by Anti-Taliban Forces (ATF). After a week of heavy skirmishing, the ATF secured one of the main ridge lines in Tora Bora, all the better for US special forces to call down B-52 air strikes on the caves and to maintain a steady but deadly round of sniping. It was enough for al-Qaeda to seek a surrender on 12 December, but only a conditional one. The US response was blunt. No surrender would be considered.

Even the al-Qaeda faithful now began to withdraw. Entering the battlefield, meanwhile, were 110 troopers of the SAS, the Regiment's largest single-battle deployment since the 1970s.

It fell to 22 SAS to raid the last fastnesses of al-Qaeda at Tora Bora. One raid, led by the Colonel and Regimental Sergeant Major of 22 SAS, lasted for five hours, as the four-man SAS teams cleared cave after cave in combat so close that at one point the RSM was fighting for his life with his K-bar knife. Outside the caves, SAS security teams eliminated any al-Qaeda fighters who fled. The SAS suffered two wounded; the al-Qaeda casualty count was 40 dead.

Three days later 40 SAS troopers, believed to be A or G Squadron, mounted another cave raid; 30 troopers entered the caves on the north side of the mountain expecting a close-quarters battle with al-Qaeda. There was some resistance, but not the usual al-Qaeda fury. Most often the SAS found as they entered the individual caves only al-Qaeda's ghosts, and they wondered where all the terrorists had gone to. The mystery was soon answered, when upwards of 100 al-Qaeda fighters emerged via a tunnel on the mountain's south side – and right into the night-sights of an eight-man SAS ambush waiting on the other side of the gorge. Despite being outnumbered ten to one, the SAS decided to engage. Disregarding normal practice, which is to conserve ammunition, the SAS team poured down fire from their two "gimpys", 7.62mm General Purpose Machine-Guns, and from their M203s (standard M16 rifles with a grenade launcher attached). Only by pinning the al-Qaeda group down could the SAS prevent their fleeing or, worse, their outflanking of the SAS position. Throughout the freezing night the eight men stayed at their position, now on weapons discipline, only firing when al-Qaeda grouped to make a break. By the time the sun cast its first shadows along the gorge next morning, all the M203 grenades had gone, so too the gimpy ammunition. Only a few mags of M203 rounds were left. Fortuitously, the rest of the squadron, having tabbed around from the north side of the mountain, then arrived and the "Siege of the White Mountains" continued for the remainder of the day. But, by dusk, the SAS was once again short on ammunition. There was only one option, to call in an air strike to land a daisy cutter on the cave entrance where al-Qaeda were holed up. There was only one problem: someone on the ground would have to highlight the target with a laser designator, and remain in position while the bomb was guided in. The kill-zone of a daisy cutter, which explodes 50 feet up in the air and sends out a seismic explosion and an immense shock wave, extends to 1,000 feet from the blast edge. All the SAS would be inside the zone, but particularly the volunteer with the laser designator.

When the blast came, all the SAS could do was crawl under whatever cover they could find, hands over their ears. It was a foretaste of Armageddon. A blasting white light and an earth-shaking boom. A hurricane rush of air. Silence.

The B-52 had lain the daisy-cutter right on the nose, To their amazement, all the SAS survived, and moved quickly to capture the stunned al-Qaeda survivors. By the Regiment's final tally, 30 al-Qaeda were captured in the siege, 27 killed and 30 wounded.

The Regiment's actions were the highlight of the Allied effort at Tora Bora, and were not enough to undo the list of

Allied inadequacies. The rivalry between the Anti-Taliban Forces for US patronage. The contempt shown by US Special Forces towards the local mujahedin. (One key ATF commander, Zahir, only learned of the initial ground assault on Tora Bora by watching CNN.) Above all the failure of CENTCOM, despite ATF warnings, to install an adequate cordon around Tora Bora.

The result was predictable. Around 3,000 al-Qaeda fighters escaped Tora Bora. And so the hunt had to begin again. By the close of January 2002 the great Allied show that assembled at Tora Bora had rolled onto other places, and on the mountain only the archaic sound of the wind in the pine trees was to be heard.